A coffee with Archangels

Isa MILLOT

A coffee with Archangels

Light Coaching for a Better Life

First edition

Publisher: Isabelle Millot 75010 Paris (France)

Print ISBN: 978-2-9584111 -1-4
E-book ISBN: 978-2-9584111-0-7

Printed in USA by Lightning Source – 1, Ingram BLVD, La Vergne TN (print on demand)

Cover: Canva

Legal deposit:
Library of Congress, Washington DC – April 2022
Bibliothèque Nationale de France – August 2022

To the beautiful white angel of my childhood…

INTRODUCTION

"Strength is having the courage to express who you are and to express Life no matter what the circumstances."
Archangel Gabriel - 2021

A few months have passed since I put the last point on the paper. You will discover that I have told my daily story alongside the Archangels with all the enthusiasm of a young author who is carrying his first great creation.
After the troubled times we have had to face, today more than ever the world needs hope and benevolence. If society is not going well, humanity is not dead. It lives on in every heart, every smile, every moment of joy, every prayer... This intimate light of consciousness rises to the sky in an eternal clamor. Silent, filled with secret hopes…
From the Highest, our heavenly friends observe us. They hear us and answer us, perhaps in a clumsy way that we do not always understand... For them

there is no such thing as deception or lies, there is no wrong road but only the one that leads to the fulfilment of our soul, to perfection.

It's when we arrive at this destination that we are ready to fully accept the blessings they have in store for us, and God knows how abundant they are...

In this life, my soul has chosen to be a psychic and to perceive the invisible. This ability to see what is not yet is sometimes misunderstood or used for dishonest purposes by individuals who care little for the harm of others.

For a long time, I considered this ability to be a real burden. The one who tries to see right is mostly considered a danger for some and a salvation for others...

The price to pay can be very high, in terms of suffering and self-denial... I've lived in hiding, in silence and discretion, convinced that I did not belong... I always remember that I am only one human among many, like you, like all...

"Feeling" didn't put me on a pedestal, quite the contrary, and didn't prevent me from making mistakes. I have known paths strewn with sharp rocks and the torture of unanswered questions. During some particularly dark days, I had the audacity to believe that God had abandoned me.

What an affront to the one who created us, who welcomes us as we are! For proof he sent me Michael, Gabriel, Raphael and Uriel. The moment I stopped believing, the moment I chose to resign myself to the way my life had turned out. A daily life devoid of color and soul...

The patience, love and knowledge they shared with me brought me face to face with the mirror.

I understood that error is a precious gift and that despite wandering, one always ends up finding the path to one's home, the path to the heart, the joy of fully existing.

Today, I walk with my soul at peace with the absolute certainty that we are the same essence, HIS essence, THEIR essence. Separation is only an illusion and self-inflicted hatred is an integral part of the masquerade.

You could have lived my life and I could have lived yours, because without knowing each other I can say that suffering very often shows a similar face when it decides to hit one of us. There's no perfect life, there's only a multitude of existences made of enigmas to decipher in order to get the best out of it...

The coaching you are about to discover is now yours. It comes from pure light, from one of those brief moments that transform us forever. One day it will return to where it came from, but in the meantime, I sincerely hope that it will bring you what you need when you need it. This is a return to the basics, to the foundations of being. It is the moment when you take off your costume and decide to make room for who you really are.

Going to meet the self is the ultimate test, the only true quest, the one that makes you invincible. Once you have completed the steps of this great adventure, you will find that the blessings you seek on the outside are in fact programmed inside you. Never lose sight of the fact that sharing makes us richer, so I hope that during this reading, through my modest earthly experience, you will find the keys you have been looking for so long...

PART 1

Childhood, angels, devils and humans

CHAPTER 1

In the beginning...

"There's nothing more beautiful than a carefree childhood still bathed in the light of the soul..."

Archangel Uriel - 2021

Who are we? Who am I?
Why am I here? Where do I belong?
In this immensity that is the world, I've asked myself this question many times. Life is like a symphony whose tempo adapts to the passing of time.
The mysterious conductors who synchronize the melody know all the notes of the score in advance. In an atmosphere of eternal repetition, they play, catching the false notes that sometimes appear, arranging new rhythms for the eternal music…

Each of us plays a piece of this music, beating the measure with ease. Hearts and bodies sway freely to the sound of this sequence which takes us from discovery to discovery before we find the Great Maestro. He may have different names, he doesn't care, if the hearts beat and vibrate in unison with HIS melody...

This melody, theirs, his, mine is dedicated to all the souls who, like me, have lost their way and are struggling to find their way back. Stumbling, falling, making mistakes, crying are not signs of weakness but an incredible strength that you don't even suspect... Do you want to join in?

I was born and raised in a small, sunny village in the south of France, a few kilometers from the ancient City of the Popes. As I write these lines, I can hear again the song of the cicadas that lulled my childhood. I remember the lavender in the garden, planted with love by my mother... A little corner of paradise on which God always keeps an eye.

God... I got to know him when I was about 4 years old. On the rare rainy days, I liked to stand at the window and watch the water fall. When the thunder roared, I would crawl into bed, wrapping myself in the blankets for protection. My mother, seeing that I was afraid, would come to me and say: *"Don't worry, the rain is the tears of the little Jesus! The thunder is God, his father, scolding him for doing something stupid".*

In my head, I had a vision of a huge man in a robe, with a long white beard. He was lecturing a little boy also dressed in white. God must have been very strong for his anger to be heard here on earth. Jesus must have been an amazing little boy for his tears to almost flood the garden.

In my childish mind I began to believe that on days when the sun was shining, I could see God's smile...

When spring came, I would take a large matchbox with holes in it to let the air in and go out into the garden to look for ladybirds. When my box was full, I would kneel in front of my mother's rose bushes, open the lid and release this treasure, which I offered to God so that he would continue to smile, and Jesus would no longer cry. I wanted to become

Jesus' friend. I wanted to comfort him; I wanted him to stop crying. I wanted to go and get the ladybirds with him so we could both give them to his daddy... When I've an idea in mind... Stubbornness, good or bad, is a character trait I've always kept…

I remember one day I emptied my school bag and put in two paper dolls I' d made. I went to my mother and asked her where God and Jesus lived. She had to take me to see them, l had a present for them. She smiled at me and said that they lived on the most beautiful cloud in the sky.
I went back to my room with my head down, very disappointed that I couldn't give my present. Send it in the mail? I didn't know how to write yet and I didn't know their address... Blow up a balloon, hang my schoolbag on it and let it fly high? I considered many possibilities but none of these plans suited me...In the end, I just looked at the sky and tried to guess which of the clouds was my friends' house.

At home, my sisters and I never received any specific religious education. My parents wanted us to make our own choices about our beliefs when we grew up. Of course, they talked to us about religion, but they didn't want to impose anything on us.

The day came when I had to face the fact that seeing God and Jesus in the flesh would be complicated... I was 7 years old... Our house was a real Noah's Ark, we had dogs, cats, birds, rodents...
I even had a little black carnivorous frog that I called Flora, because it reminded me of the shimmering flowers found in the jungle.

Nearby, there was a couple of neighbors who had a sheepdog. It was late afternoon and from the kitchen window my sisters and I saw the dog owner standing at our gate. We went to get my mother to tell her that the lady next door was there. Things were not going well between my parents and these people, and suddenly I started to tremble.
In my ears I could hear "Snoopy, snoopy", the name of the little Burmese cat that was part of our happy pack of four-legged friends. I can see my mother gesticulating in the distance. The discussion

between her and the neighbor looked lively. She had asked us to stay in the house, so I went to prostrate myself on the living room couch, my heart sinking, the name Snoopy buzzing in my head.

When mum came back, her face showed a mixture of anger and sadness. Something in me knew something bad had happened... Snoopy had gone into the neighbor's garden, the sheepdog saw him and wanted to protect his territory... Snoopy lost the battle...

Our cat was dead, and I cried my eyes out. I didn't really know what death was yet, I had never experienced it directly. We went to the cemetery to bring flowers from time to time, but I thought it was different for humans. Animals could not die, these beings who give us so much love can only be eternal…

Why did death have to hurt so much? Why was it sad? I wish God had taken me in his big arms to comfort my childish heart...

I never liked visits to the cemetery, my ears would ring, my head would nearly explode, and I would see people who scared me… I hoped Snoopy would come home. My mother told me that the angels had come to take him to God's heaven. But then, if Snoopy was with God, Jesus and the angels, he was bound to come back, like the sun and the rain... I tried to convince myself of this, but in my heart, something told me otherwise...

The days passed, and the absence continued... When I returned from school, I inspected the house in the hope of seeing him back... One night in bed I hid under the duvet and asked God if Snoopy was okay. I hoped the voice would answer me... but nothing!
Sleep took me away. In what I thought was a dream, I was sucked into a shiny whirlpool. I couldn't tell how big it was. A meter? A kilometer? I don't know how far it covered; it went very fast. When I arrived, I fell from a great height.
Strangely enough, the fall didn't hurt, I couldn't feel my body. I landed in a meadow with soft green grass. In the distance I could see a mountain with a cloudy top. From the blue sky there was no sound, no birds, no planes... Silence, peace... I stood up; in

the distance I saw two figures coming towards me. The first one was giant with huge wings, graceful looking.
The white light coming from him was dazzling, a bit like looking at the sun too long on a summer afternoon... An angel, majestic, beautiful, with a kind face... His appearance reflected Love and that is what I think this feeling should look like. Beside him was a tiny beige and brown shape with a golden halo... Snoopy!

I couldn't move or speak, if I tried no sound came out of my mouth, my legs wouldn't respond. They came closer, so the angel held out his giant arm to show me Snoopy. He was beautiful, just like the last time I had seen him. I was fine, soothed, I didn't want to leave, stay with them in this corner of Paradise... Except that I made my way back… I was pushed into the whirlpool and back into my bed.
I woke up sweating, disappointed to have left this wonderful place. I knew where God lived now...
Of course, I didn't tell anyone about this. Not even my family!

As for the school, I saw no point in talking about it there. I was already being mocked by the other kids, and I would have taken a lot of punishment if they had known that...

So, I wanted to keep the memory of this great white angel all to myself... I liked him, a lot... I wanted him to be my friend too... And he was! In better and in worse! If later my naivety was abused and I had the sadness of knowing the ravages of lies, this time my mother had not lied. God lived in heaven, Jesus too and Snoopy was with them. All was fine…

But in my head, it was a mess. The strange experience I had undergone changed things in my daily life and my perceptions. I was also curious to know more. From a very young age, my parents talked to us about everything. They wanted us to be more open-minded and to go beyond what we learned at school. They were not practicing but they liked to tell us about the great facts of Catholicism. I was delighted to hear about Jesus, Mary, God, heaven, angels... This brought me closer to my beautiful white angel, the one in the mountains. In secret, I would take my parents' encyclopedia's and spend hours reading them to quench my thirst for divine knowledge.

In Provence, there is no shortage of places steeped in history. This region is full of ancient vestiges where cultures and religions mix. I loved the Sunday walks, when my father would get out the car to take us to the Saint-Michel de Frigolet abbey. Michael, my parents' favorite Archangel, the guardian of our home...

I've kept a special affection for this abbey. The atmosphere of the churches calms me. The mystery and secrets of their walls create a climate of trust where one can feel the abandonment of hearts that have placed their fate in the hands of the Lord. For me, it was the kingdom of God! A warm and welcoming place, where no difference exists because we are always welcome as we are. No firsts, no lasts, only love.

The voice that told me Snoopy had died became more regular. Her messages were clear and concise.

Now that I am an adult, I am sure that my beautiful white angel is no stranger to these dazzling intuitions that have been passed on to me during my life.
I was a shy and lonely child. At school it was worse! I had big attention problems and going to class meant deep boredom. The subjects that interested me were French, history, drawing...

The teachers didn't waste any time, they labelled me as a dumb kid from the start. I didn't make it easy for them either. During school hours, my beautiful white angel visited me to explain the lessons differently. I started talking to him out loud without the slightest concern for other people or teacher. I liked to learn differently, so I found it difficult to fit into a school system that didn't want children like me.

I can say that my beautiful angel and I did the four hundred tricks at school! I assure you, it was never mean, I wouldn't have tolerated it, and neither would he!

No one wanted to play with me at break time. Fortunately, my angel introduced some new friends to me. They were invisible but I didn't care. We played marbles, hopscotch, anything I wanted.
They were bright and always friendly, they smiled at me... I was secure with them, protected as in a soap bubble. I loved them so much... In those moments, my beautiful white angel was present at our games. He stood at a distance, surrounding us all with his big wings.

Their presence helped me to bear the nastiness of the other children and teachers. As well as playing with me, my new friends talked to me. They would tell me things that I didn't necessarily understand, and they always came true. Thanks to them, I knew if the day was going to be good or bad, what event was going to happen. I knew my school results even before I had the corrected paper in front of me. During tests, they would sometimes whisper a few right answers to me...
At home, I knew when trouble was coming. I couldn't say anything to my parents, how could I

explain it to them? Would they have believed me anyway?
All this made me even more sensitive. I liked to be in my room with my books, soaking up beautiful stories. Was I weird? Without a doubt!
I liked to walk along the paths and stop to pick flowers for my mother... I liked to blow on dandelions and watch their petals fly up to the sky...
I loved to take in lost animals because I couldn't bear to see them alone without a family... It was my childhood Paradise, and nothing could take it away from me!

I was met with incomprehension from my family. On the advice of the school, my mother took me to a psychologist for a while. The sessions were weird. The therapist would ask me to draw, which I tried to do, but I think he didn't quite understand my scribbles...
Sometimes I was bored so I would lie on the couch and not say a word. I would look with interest at the books piled up on the shelf... Other times my beautiful white angel would appear behind the

therapist's back. I laughed heartily at this heavenly joke while the psychologist looked at me incredulously...

This good man felt he could do nothing for me. He preferred to let it go, he told my mother that I didn't need any more sessions. His diagnosis came down hard and fast... Depression! I carried this error of judgement like a ball and chain for over twenty years... I often cried for this world I didn't understand. Only my friends in the light could console me. They helped me to soften the injustices I suffered. On the outside, my tears were linked to depression. The reason was simple: I was not in the norm, that's all!

No one ever tried to break through my shell. It was more comfortable to say that my sadness came from being fat and inadequate. With my bright friends anything was possible. They taught me to see the best in others, because despite everything I loved people. I love the life that springs from them, their laughter, their smiles... except that I didn't have the instructions to fit in with them... I could never explain this reason to anyone until today!

CHAPTER 2

On the road to spirituality

"Being spiritual transcends belief and opinion, there is always a way for those who seek the truth of God"
Archangel Gabriel - 2021

I grew up, as best I could... Adolescence was a difficult period in my life. The atmosphere at home was fluctuating, with some ups and many downs. My new life as a schoolgirl and the reality of it had nothing to do with the glamorous and hectic life of TV heroes. Sometimes I envied these young, hip fictional characters who were surrounded by loyal and popular friends.

As far as I'm concerned… I had trouble fitting in, I was too babyish, not rebellious enough for the others. I didn't skip school, I didn't smoke, at least not yet, I was a fan of boy bands, I wasn't the

prettiest and I had this childish mentality that was a stain on the landscape. At 12/13 years old, I still liked to play with my dolls or spend hours in front of my television playing endless video games.
In fact, fashions passed by at lightning speed and I remained faithful to what I liked... All the conditions were there for this to pose a huge problem socially.

My entry into the world of adolescence changed me all the same. My perceptions became different. I found myself between two worlds. On the one hand I refused to let go of the childhood that lived inside me, and on the other I felt such a need to fit in that I found my childishness ridiculous...
My friends in the light must have felt this beginning of an inner fracture. The voice that had informed me so many times over the past few years was manifesting itself differently.

I could no longer hear it whispering distinctly in my ear. It was speaking in a different way. I no longer received omens for a specific situation, for example, but I could perceive people and things. I was getting information about the past, the present or the future... It was rather destabilizing... Leaving aside the spiritual and frightening aspect that this provoked in a girl of my age, the strangest thing was the physical sensation that accompanied each of these omens.

Each time, I felt a great suction in my solar plexus, as if it was opening in two. Bell-like sounds and crystalline vibrations would gradually rise into my mind.

I think the thing that distressed me the most was how to accurately translate the messages I received. I found it incredible that I was able to transform these sounds into words without difficulty; whereas at school I closed myself off to understanding and my grades were not above average.

The loving presences that used to accompany me were becoming rarer.

These lights with infinite and universal knowledge must have sensed the emerging duality I was experiencing. Without realizing it, I turned my back on them and began to deny my childhood values to blend in. Adolescence is a world of appearance and fierce competition. The law of the strongest and of young, overinflated egos. I realize that living in my light bubble had its advantages. At home in particular, my proximity to my beautiful white angel had made me miss some disturbing facts...

The place where we lived was built on the site of an old factory that had been destroyed by fire. The story goes that the employees were still inside when the tragedy occurred.
It was not difficult to understand that our house was the cradle of suffering souls, gone too soon and too fast. The den of unfulfilled destinies... However, my mother loved her house, which she maintained like a precious jewel. I must admit that I was sometimes afraid in certain rooms, especially after dark. Apart from that, nothing strange ever happened to me. My two sisters, by contrast, were the victims of a few bad jokes...

The most emblematic room in the house was the large living room, which you had to walk through

to get to the staircase that went to the first floor. This staircase was quite steep and very high. More than once, my sisters were "pushed" down the stairs... These untimely falls could have caused serious damage.
Thank God, nothing serious ever happened except for a few scares... At first, one could have thought that they were clumsy... The children run without necessarily paying attention. Except that my sisters' explanation was always the same. They hadn't slipped, they weren't running, they said they felt a force behind their backs that pushed them off balance...

My parents always believed in spirits, ghosts, negative waves... The superstition they had could take on enormous proportions. In their eyes, everything was either black or white. The usual mentality was to see the glass as half empty... Besides, between my first experiences of light, what I saw, and certain words spoken at home, we were in two different moods... I don't blame them; family is one of the most important things in life and my parents did their best for their three daughters. But it was not easy for me to be in an atmosphere of renunciation. When a problem arose, I often heard that it was God's fault because he abandoned us or that there was a curse on our house...

This kind of talk helped to reinforce the spiritual duality that was being created in me… I was lost because what I had experienced when Snoopy died, the company of my white angel, the omens that proved to be true, were all real. Next to this, there was the reality of life passing by, where one galley after another followed...

When you're a kid, you imagine that your parents are always right. As for me, I saw mine struggling day by day to sort things out, so their lamentations were justified. More than once, I asked God and my friends to help us. Did they? Honestly, I was too young to remember!

I don't hide the fact that I resented them. Through them I received information I didn't need, but when I needed them, they turned a deaf ear... Today I am ashamed to have been so unfair. Some of the subtleties of heaven and earthly incarnation still escaped me... They also did their best, but I did not have the necessary distance to understand it...

In their constant defeatism, they concluded that our misfortunes came from the house itself. More than likely when you knew the history of the property. The memory of the earth and the walls causes just as much energetic damage as the entities… Cross-referencing the events, between the constant difficulties and the recurrent falls down the stairs, my parents' conclusion was legitimate.

And that's when my spiritual life took a new turn. Through an encounter that confronted me with a judgmental spirituality, made of rules, codes and injunctions... The dark side of a spirituality, which under the guise of benevolence, only feeds the ego of those who put it into practice!

Not knowing what to do, my parents called a healer to try to understand what was happening in the house. She came with her equipment, performed various "tests" and gave her verdict: there were many telluric waves and suffering souls that could not be removed. She gave some advice on how to lighten the energies and began to observe each of us.

I have never liked the great airs that some people give themselves. When they leave the suspense hanging before, they speak to make sure they captivate their audience... Suddenly she announced emphatically that my father and younger sister had the gift of healing. My other sister would become a great psychic because she had incredible power...
For the grand inspection, only my mother and I were left.
When it was my turn, the healer barely looked at me and quickly said that I had some "gifts" to predict the future. That's it, nothing more!

As she left, she raved about my older sister's pseudo-powers, again predicting a future of fame, money and recognition... Fortunately, no man holds the truths of world in his hands... If this lady was convinced of the words and judgements she had that day, the future did not prove her right… The fact remains that this visit had a negative impact on the family beliefs. The feeling of superiority of some who felt invested with a divine mission began to seriously parasitize the little harmony that existed. Personally, the healer's reaction and contemptuous words challenged me. If I only had a few "gifts" to predict the future, it meant that my light experience was meaningless...

I didn't know any more and I couldn't talk about it because the spotlight was on the one who was to become the incredible oracle... I speak of all this completely without bitterness or jealousy.

For a long time, I've been saddened to see that the professions of helping others lead to major drifts among practitioners and consultants.

Blunt judgements are unfortunately commonplace, whereas these activities require humility and discernment. What happened to me then? The transformation was underway... I left my friends in the light and started a new occupation: drawing cards!

My first game was rudimentary. It was a Tarot deck offered in a magazine dedicated to horoscopes.
It was there that I discovered that it was necessary to respect certain methods of drawing and especially that there were an incalculable number of associations of cards. Visually, this Tarot displeased me to no end, but the thing that opened the door to the specter of fear was practice.
The "definite" draws and omens were in total contradiction with the messages I was receiving from the invisible.
I couldn't understand why a card association was limited to saying one thing when in my ears I was hearing the opposite.

Tarots, Oracles or any other divination tools have a rather striking visual aspect and when you are a novice, you tend to refer to the established rules. Tarot cards are hard and implacable, for me they have always represented a fate from which one cannot escape. I think my spiritual breakthrough officially began there. I drew the cards in panic fear of what they would announce. My friends in the

light continued to help me from afar, but I could no longer make sense of things.
I had difficulty believing in my own truth and my inner listening. I had developed the belief that without cards I was nothing... These anxieties swept away the light of my inner world in one fell swoop.

I was 14 and lonely. On the plus side, I was curious. I thought there might be other people like me who could calm me down, explain things to me, give me advice.
The healer's visit had one advantage; it made my family want to meet people with "abilities". I don't like this term to describe a person with developing intuition! I find it nauseatingly pretentious. I'm not discrediting anyone because spiritual experience is intimate and personal. Only, for me, having abilities implies that there is a handful of hand-picked people. We all have natural predispositions, there are as many forms of mediumship as there are humans. Everyone has potential to reveal, without exception! Spirituality is supposed to be an environment of tolerance and love, not an endless

battle of egos. Let's think about Jesus, before he was elevated to the rank of model, he was one of the greatest misunderstood in history. So, you can be a chosen one and have a hard life...

I looked for mentors. It was written that those who would have this role would arrive later at my journey...

At 14, my "model" at the time called S. She was also a card reader and already had some experience... Except that her readings reflected the errors of those who imagine themselves to be invested with a divine power that makes them superior. One should not expect any positivity from her. She was brittle, judgmental and always predicted catastrophic events...

Experience has taught me that clairvoyance should be used to guide and not to impose anything. It is an enormous responsibility to establish certainties about the possible outcome of a situation... Errors of interpretation are possible, and the fulfillment of predictions isn't an exact science.

We're only human... But S. didn't see it that way. For her, clairvoyance was a way of crushing the other person!

She would announce horrors bluntly, completely forgetting that she was dealing with a human being in the grip of doubt or anxiety!

The worst thing was that when she saw her client unsettled, she would say, without any empathy, that this was fate.

She treated me the same way... She took advantage of my youth and my naivety to take away all hope for a positive future. She knew everything, had all the answers... She told me that people would never trust me because of my young age...

If the cards announced a message, the fatality of the negative event would automatically prevail... I was even more afraid! Fortunately, time and my friends the Archangels have taught me that the cards have their limits.

This is true for all divinatory tools. They are only doors to the invisible and you never know who is behind them despite all the precautions you take.

You must know how to take some and leave some! The world of light, God, Archangels, angels, ascended masters, guides, the departed... Only they are infallible in the answers they give because they only support and bring additional knowledge to what our soul already knows.

The worst mistake I made was to stop believing in my luminous friends, in my beautiful white angel. I was in awe of S., her ease and what I thought was immense knowledge.

After that, my spiritual journey was built on a pattern of all kinds of superstitions. The guidance that helped me remained, assisting me when I practiced clairvoyance. In 23 years of practice, I have navigated in troubled waters, dominated by doubt and lack of confidence. My consultants were happy with my predictions, yet I was conducting my consultations with a sinking feeling...

I was always afraid of being wrong, even though I never let on. I wouldn't generalize it to spirituality because that's how the world works, but making mistakes means being weak. I've always had a very different approach to cards than S. did. With those who have placed their trust in me, I've always tried to be neutral and honest.

A psychic doesn't know everything! Far from it!
I've always found it ridiculous to entertain hopes to fill in the blanks. It's more interesting to provide keys that really help the other person to move forward.
Some truths must remain hidden. If they eventually come out, they're not always good to tell... Not everyone evolves in the same way or at the same speed. We must learn to distinguish between what people WANT to hear and what they're READY to hear.

No matter what anxieties were invading my life, my line was clear on this point. My role isn't to pass on my discomfort to others but to accompany them with kindness. A person must live his or her experience. We can think that certain choices that are made aren't the right ones, everyone is free to make their own opinions…

Let's remain kind and respectful whatever happens, we're not tyrannical little leaders or oppressors!
Life has hurt me so much; I don't see the point of taking cowardly revenge by putting down someone who is doing badly... A smile, a kind word or an extended hand can do wonders...

My first encounter with human spirituality extinguished the light of my childhood.
The clairvoyance opened a Pandora's box that took me years to close... The ego, this companion of misfortune maintains low beliefs and fixed ideas... That friend of fear...
Who, through the medium of a card game, has managed to engulf me in the quicksand of inner struggle. Yet I loved my job. I always considered myself a people's psychic. Helping others has always been a priority in my life and I think that's what blocked me with some of the spiritual encounters I had.
Deep down, there was still a little flame living inside me. The reason that encouraged me to continue in esotericism was the memory of the love I received

from the world of light as a child. I wanted to share this love at all costs to avoid suffering for others. When I joined spiritual circles, my idealism made me believe that I would find people like me, eager for love and light.

I saw myself brandishing my sword to defend great causes and protect the weakest from injustice... But we are only flesh and blood beings, so don't blame anyone.

I had my own experiences; I've met great people who have taught me a lot...

I've also been disappointed, I've been confronted with a misplaced elitism, with people whose knowledge was used as an excuse to have power over the other... Despite everything, I continued my way. I studied the subjects that interested me. I was looking for answers, I wanted to know. Experts, testimonies, shared experiences...

I read, listened, analyzed and from all these truths and contradictions that flashed before my eyes, one thing became clear: What about the opinion of heaven in all this?

After all, it never takes sides when you think about it... Not once has God, an ascended master, an angel, manifested himself in the middle of a spiritual conference or workshop.
Never do they come out and say "Yes, this is the way to do it!" or "No, you're doing it all wrong!".
The collective miraculous apparitions have always taken place before groups of normal people, whose faith is unshakeable. This is irrefutable proof that possessing mediumship or other abilities does not confer any privilege in the eyes of God and his troops! He loves us all equally, whatever we are!

We are only submitting to human interpretations in the end... The sharing of knowledge or experience should only serve our inspiration for the purpose of personal elevation. Spirituality is a springboard to the knowledge of our full potential. It should not in any way establish codes of right and wrong. Life takes care soon enough to place us in turn in the judge's chair and the dock.
For a long time, I tortured myself with the reductive precepts drawn from certain teachings. Mass beliefs

that if we don't act in a certain way, we will never get what we want or if things get stuck, it's because we are not pure enough or too polluted by evil...

I never used to ask myself what I was going to do... My quest for answers coupled with selfish opinions was widening the gap of " I've got a shitty life and it's all my fault because my karma is rotten, I've got a debt to pay, I'm victim of witchcraft, curses… Spirituality, instead of liberating me, ended up putting me in the cage of guilt-inducing "truths".... The world needs inspirational spirits who touch hearts and souls. They are to be found in all walks of life, not just the spiritual ones, so let's not fall into the trap of stifling thought, for wherever you go, the light forces are ready to help you...

CHAPTER 3

The Evil forces

"The one you call the devil is the side of deep knowledge you don't want to reveal. The lower instincts that your nature strives to dominate. The dark side you don't want to admit."
Archangel Michael - 2021

God wins all suffrages in the hearts of men. The troubled relationship we may have with him, and his benevolent envoys doesn't call into question his supreme leadership of the good.

But what about the Devil? The antithesis of our beloved Almighty, he is the undisputed face of evil. Moreover, if God is confronted with faith crises among his most ardent supporters, the same cannot be said about the Devil...

Fearful and dreaded, this entity of all superstitions has the worst reputation. A truly black sheep of the flock, his name is associated with all the misdeeds committed in the world. However, the horror that he inspires fascinates. When understanding God seems beyond our powers, the Devil has no trouble luring us into the nets of the morbid, into the very heart of those shadows that we reject with great moralizing. Although I have known suffering, mockery, malice, betrayal or blockage, I have never really been conscious of what evil means in its definition. Where does it begin, after all? Where it stops? As a child, I had no idea that it could come and meet me… Some days were worse than others, that's all... S.'s strange mentoring made me anxious, insecure, always in fear of the Devil and his host of troublemakers.

Oh sure, I was nurtured with stories of his sinister prowess and attempts to enslave people through the ages... God's greatness wouldn't be what it is if we didn't talk about his opposite…

At the age of 15, I understood the extent of damages that are caused in the name of this one who is a reference of absolute evil. Do we know him well, this ghost that haunts us? My parents, my sisters and I had moved to a new house, closer to my father's work.

The family atmosphere deteriorated over the years. A permanent sadness engulfed our broken family. My father was nothing but anger and screaming, and my mother was nothing but grief...

My school results were getting lower, and I couldn't believe that everything would be alright. I refused to see my beautiful white angel and my friends of light. I spent days in my bedroom, listening to music to escape the oppressive atmosphere. I couldn't stand hearing that God didn't love us, that we were damned...

Such an unhelpful context only strengthened the kind of unhealthy fascination I had for S… Me, the insecure teenager, the indigent parent of spirituality whose only experience was his curiosity and his childish lights... In my eyes, S.'s bitter speeches were the gospel!

Not satisfied to dominate others with her negative clairvoyance, she saw fit to add one more skill to her credit: practice of witchcraft. From then on, her disdain for mankind only increased. Money spells, love potions and snake powders became a reason to alienate one's fellow man to her cause... God himself was unworthy of a look!

I saw her, harshly deciding the other's fate, thinking she was untouchable. My heart broke at the sight of those whom she described as Gogo's rushing to her home in search of illusion for want of truth. All this made me think. I was not unaware of the devil's existence, he must have been lurking somewhere anyway, but I always believed he was the big loser in the battle.

S.'s actions made me doubt and shattered the fragments of conviction that still survived in me. I was revolted by her dubious practices because I always thought that one must have fallen very low to indulge in practices that took away all free will, on the other hand she was getting results... God loves us dearly, he gives us the choice, but the forces with which S. allied herself gave exactly what the people wanted... So many easy promises to satisfy desperate egos... I then began to be conscious that the evil actions of humans are perhaps worse than the work of the Devil!

God has spread love and light on earth, his rival has added vice, each one chooses his camp finally.

The magic that S. used to conquer is not a directive of the devil. He put this tool among many others at the disposal of our illusions except that we have the choice. To use a Peau de Chagrin to get out of situations we don't like...

Is this worth it? Of course, if we consider things from a purely material point of view.

Like Faust or Ambrosio, who were consumed by the torments of dissatisfaction, we get everything we ask for without considering for a moment that there is always a reverse side to the coin... With the forces of evil, you can forget about after-sales service, you get the goods as they are!

Witnessing all this only reinforced the fear in my heart. The omens on the cards had locked me into an image of fatal outcomes but discovering this other aspect of spirituality only tightened up the bars of the prison. I naively thought that only God could intervene to help us, because he is the strongest... S. proved to me that humans can thwart God's plans. Temporarily of course, but when he does, it is very unpleasant!

Everyone dreads the devil's mischief, but isn't it mankind that disturbs his sinister tranquility?
In my life, characters like S. have succeeded one another, because alas, the spiritual and esoteric universe is full of such specimens.
Beware, I am not generalizing because they don't represent the majority. However, they emulate enough to attract attention and put spotlights on them… In the name of good, I saw people judged, broken, destroyed, deprived of hope in moments when they only needed help…

Under the pretext of bringing light to humanity, Jesus, Alchemists, descendants of Atlantis and other reincarnations of historical characters, inflate their ego in search of recognition so that the flaws of their malaise are not revealed. They feed a public eager

for sensationalism and ready to believe anything so long as it makes them dream... The Forces of Evil exist, indeed! And many practitioners have fought them relentlessly.
Carrying the torch of light to illuminate their battles while forgetting that they went to find the Devil in his lair...
I've known blockages and failures, the few times I asked for advice, I was always served on a platter with spells, omens of loneliness, death, curses.... The absent are always wrong and it is very convenient to lynch Satan in the public square in order to make him responsible for the dark parts of our souls!

The dark forces exist, and they are like human relationships that are based solely on appearances. We condemn our own terrors in others because they seem less inaccessible than our lights!
Devil, his demons and men... I saw them in action. Contrary to what we believe, it is not the malicious ones who turn out to be dangerous. Beware of false guides and false lights, because in their wake the scent of Sulphur is sometimes present...

Even if I feared them, to better circumvent them, one must learn to know them.
Learning about the tools used by the weak and cowardly did not give me the advantage... But it did give me an understanding of some of their motivations.

Devil, demons, humans, same fight!
Their strength is proportional to the power we give them! With my persistent fear and repeated anxieties, I believe I have been bringing oxygen to the pyre of the evil forces for a good twenty years.
I invited them in without realizing it, through my inner turmoil I went looking for them, and they were quick to squat my existence by attracting people and events into my life that pulled me down...
If they hold our hand on the road of the ego and the choices that feed them, I also know by experience that they have their limits and that their intervention doesn't last in time. There's no shadow without light, otherwise life would not be what it is. Crossing paths with ghosts, demons, vampires or

succubae are just challenges to overcome. They are names we put on faces we are unable to see.

So consumed by the darkness that blinds us, we almost forget that it is under the close watch of the light.
The earth is a vast playground for these so-called malevolent energies, but the Big Boss knows when to ring the bell to call back his lost lambs...
The game ends, the party is over, it's time to go home safe and sound!

CHAPTER 4

Did you say Miracle?

"The miracle doesn't follow any logic; it holds its essence in the surrender..."
Archangel Uriel - 2021

The hope of a miracle is a secret common to all hearts. The popular unconscious defines it as the rapid and unexpected resolution of a problem that had no solution.
I myself have long defined the miracle in this way. The imprint of deep evil never lasts, and God knows how to call for arbitration to bring his lost sheep back into the fold. A fulfilled life is made up of successive shadows and lights.
So, when the end of a tunnel gives us a glimpse of the dawn of change, what is the face of the miracle? The Big Boss' whistle blew for me in 2011. I was 27 years old, and my young adult life didn't quite turn

out the way I'd imagined it younger. As a kid, I saw myself as a cook, a make-up artist, a lawyer.
Creating and defending, two words that have always resonated positively with me.

Unfortunately, my duality did not help me to make the right choices in life. I chose the path of parties, artificial paradises and the mirages of this world, hoping to find my place in it.
My childhood dreams were far away and turning away from God's reason led me from disaster to disaster. I don't victimize myself. Growing older and experiencing a major spiritual transformation through the Archangels taught me to step back. In all objectivity, most events that I've considered harmful stem from my own responsibility.

My "voice", the one that helped me with guidance to help others, struggled to be heard when it came to me. It warned me, that's all it did…
It was easier for me to hide behind fear and superstition, so that I had good reason to harbor unnecessary resentments and revolts. Pretexts, more

pretexts, to justify the tortuous paths I was taking…
That year, I was confronted with the cruelest form of psychological abuse that can exist: narcissistic perversion.
A classic case of repeating patterns. Wanting to find my place at all costs and conditioning myself in the belief that I was useless and invisible could only put me in a position of inferiority towards the outside world.
I lived in the same house as my oppressor and I was tired of never doing enough, of living in conflict, in devaluation... I was on the verge of cracking under the pressure of reproach and verbal abuse.

I decided to go and see my father, in the South of France. Since his divorce from my mother two years earlier, he was no longer the same man, he had become jovial, cheerful.
It's crazy to see such a difference in a human being. When two people who don't understand each other try to stay together, it irreparably widens the gap between them. Growing up with parents who don't like each other plays a major role in how much you

love yourself. One of the roots of the evil, or not... How did God decide to call me back into his flock? By involving old acquaintances!

My beautiful white angel and my light friends decided to break down the door of the room I'd locked them in. When I arrived at my father's house, I wanted to take stock of the meaning of my life, or rather its lack of meaning. My private life, my professional life... I couldn't find my way.

Of course, practicing clairvoyance allowed me to find some comfort despite the fact I couldn't protect myself. My empathy was so strong that I didn't want to see others suffer, trying to help them as best I could be my way of redeeming my own mistakes.
I was paralyzed by fear of my own fate and absorbed the energies of others, believing myself strong enough to carry it all... I was suffocating and did not know where to turn to change the course of fate…
I enjoyed spending time with my father and have true discussions with him. When he was still living

with us, he was a cold man, not very expressive. Now he was calm, relaxed, at peace. Despite this, I couldn't help but feel my heart sinking when I looked at him. I sensed something serious, but I put it down to fear.
My father, that rock...

It was a spring day and I still think about what happened... We were driving together, an ordinary trip like many others. To get home, we crossed the main street of a village where the speed limit is 30km/h. In his old age, my father stopped being a driving fool and was even more careful.
I was sitting on the passenger side when suddenly I see another car coming at full speed in front of us. It was dangerously close. Given the road's configuration, it was an inevitable crash! I turned my head to look at my father and for some reason my attention was attracted to the steering wheel. In a split second, a huge white figure invaded the cabin and turned the steering wheel a few centimeters to the right... This move caused our car to veer off course and start driving on a tiny piece of

pavement. I saw the other car go by and continue its mad dash to crash into the wall of a house a few meters away...
I looked at my father, he was pale as death, shocked. When he came to his senses, he raised his arms to the sky and cried out *"Thank the Great Architect of the Universe!"*

He wasn't wrong, everyone calls him something different, but our Big Boss blew his whistle and sent my beautiful white angel to our rescue... He was the magician who saved us from death!
My father was overcome with fear, he had lost all his driving reflexes so he could never have reacted so quickly.
My beautiful white angel... I would recognize his special vibratory signature if I closed my eyes... He's like that great love that you never forget when you're lucky enough to find it... Without him, it was the final clap...
It took me years to understand the depth of this miracle... After the shock, I knew that I would have to make certain decisions and stick to them. I always

intellectualized things to the extreme, my inner demons didn't help me to clear my head and self-confidence can't be regained in a snap... I was angry at myself for my ungrateful attitude and ignorance towards my bright loves...

I returned to Paris and settled my accounts with my narcissistic pervert. This was not done gently; I was greeted with a shower of blows and insults, but I held on...
What's the worst that can happen when you've already survived...

Eight months later, Our Father called mine back to him... It was seven days before Christmas that the lights went out to take him to other skies. When I learned of his death, I thought of that spring day that almost marked our farewell to this world.
Why did he grant us life if he was going to take it from us later?
Sometimes the Divine's proofs of love seem like injustice in the eyes of men. And God knows how unfair I found it... Once again, the guidance, that

"voice" inside me was right. But no matter how great our talents or abilities, we're very little in the end. We never fully understand the exact content of the dialogues from heaven and the messages of love that are given to us.

The day before he died, my father phoned me. I was busy at the time and couldn't answer. I promised myself I would call him back the next day, I didn't have time to make the call...

What about the miracle then?

Uriel would later teach me that the miracle isn't found where one looks for it.

The miracle isn't always the brilliant manifestation that we expect, the one that satisfies the ego. In truth, the miracle is to be aware that even if we feel alone, there's somewhere, in this dimension or in another, something or someone to love us and remind us that we deserve to live.

The miracle is to adopt the language of the heart and not to miss any phone call because nobody knows what the next day will be like... The miracle is having the courage to dare to be yourself no matter what the circumstances. Assuming who you are is accepting to carry the magic. To remove our blinders in order to perceive the heavenly reality that blesses us with its beneficial energy.

The problem with our belief in the miracle comes from our ever-increasing external expectations, driven by a sense of competitiveness that we cultivate despite ourselves.
The society that gives us birth conditions us in the prison of selfish comforts. Dissatisfaction and a sense of failure are increasingly present. Unexpected successes are a guarantee of our worth, we see in them the divine manna finally opened, rewarding us for our efforts, whereas the real miracle comes from that strength of love that we can experience in all circumstances...
For every man is a miracle...

CHAPTER 5

The main lines of life

"Among the multitude of choices, you will always find the way. Cross the void without fear, it's part of the movement."
Archangel Gabriel - 2021

The logbook of a life is punctuated by ambivalence. Answering the call to change is not easy. It is a question of time, willpower, energy... Waking up, opening your eyes and starting over is easier said than done. Spending your life building and trying to be satisfied with what you have.
To feel in your heart the irrepressible desire for somewhere else, to hear it calling your name and not know what to do...

The years following my father's death were a succession of routines and repetitive actions. Metro, job, nap, that was my rhythm... Getting out of the circle of narcissistic perversion was a kind of feat that I never thought myself capable of.

I tried to think less about the things that distressed me in order to keep myself in a routine that I thought was comfortable.

My life was not the one I'd dreamed of, and I think I'd come to accept the idea that I wasn't cut out for it. However, life is full of great moments and breaking points... I was there!

I worked a lot and in my spare time I did my clairvoyance consultations.

It was a form of resistance, like clockwork, to prevent me from asking myself questions. If there are facts of free will over which we can have control thanks to our choices, certain main lines of life cannot escape us...

I had both feet in the past, my mind in the future, and the present I was content to walk through under general anesthesia. However, I felt my body torn between two energies. The first one I knew very well. It was my old friend the belief that had accustomed me to what I imagined myself to be: the

one who struggled to change, to please others and to conform to what was expected of me.
The result: a total lack of self-confidence, an inability to assert myself and people who took advantage of my kindness.
The other energy I was equally familiar with was the light and its representatives. Whatever happens, it always finds its way in... I
n the form of resurgences, I started to become aware of the reasons for my life blocks.
Of course, being conditioned in belief, I started to freak out and imagine the worst because I couldn't see any solutions to this.

Letting the world see what I am seemed impossible. It meant having enough courage to live something different, but I didn't know myself if I was capable of it or not...
Fear of mockery, rejection, indifference, contempt... I had to face these reactions so much that in my eyes I could only be received like this by others... To protect myself, I was always very demanding with myself. I imagined that if I did this, I would not be

blamed for anything. I was wrong... It opened the door to abuse... Getting the mirror in your face can hurt!

This sort of energetic cataclysm that was taking place inside me damaged my dynamism. My body gave out and fatigue took hold of me, leading me into endless nights where I hoped that no one would interrupt the sleep I needed…

Solitude was my refuge. I started an introspective process that was not objective because it was based on my deep-rooted fears. For the first time in my life, I admitted loud and clear that I needed help... Did I find myself facing one of these main lifelines? One of those transformations you can't escape? More than likely! The event that woke me up was not as chivalrous as those movie scenes I loved so much, but it had the merit of seriously challenging me.

It was 2020 and I was aimlessly surfing the Internet. It's amazing how a simple search engine can be an inexhaustible source of information and inspiration.

Scrolling through my screen without much interest, an image suddenly caught my eye.
Among the astronomical number of images offered by the browser, this one was, as it were, "magnetic". I clicked on it to enlarge. It was a representation of the four Archangels: Michael, Gabriel, Raphael and Uriel. The caption on the photo stated that it was a mosaic in St John's Church, Warminster, England. Totally captivated, my eyes could not take my eyes off the image.

I began to tremble and feel a wave of love that was unlike any earthly feeling... Nothing existed anymore, only me and the four Archangels on my computer screen. My contemplation had been going on for a while when I suddenly heard a soft voice whispering in my ear, *"Write us!"*

I was used to "my voice", those bell-like sounds that I could translate into words, but this vibration was audible and different. I recorded the image; something told me that I had to keep it close to me and I heard again: *"Write us"*. In my legendary stubbornness, I always tried to ignore the signs that were beneficial to me. Except that now my intuition took over. It was now or never, and I couldn't afford to doubt this sign!

"Write us" ... This phrase echoed in my skull for days. I was so steeped in the spiritual conditioning that kept me in line that it seemed unlikely that the Archangels would make this request of me, who was not the most exemplary of the flock...
I feel such respect for these four iconic figures!

They're the only ones who bring people together, regardless of their beliefs, their religion. Their beloved presence is never questioned and is not subject to the slightest disagreement in a world permanently divided.
Life had taught me to keep some rationality so as not to lose my head or go off on dangerous experiences. I've seen too many people lose their heads in the name of good and go off course, caught in the trap of the human being who thinks he is strong enough to control certain forces.

Michael, Gabriel, Raphael, Uriel... Four of God's top ministry people... I should have felt honored, but I didn't. Instead, I felt unworthy and ashamed of who I was...
So-called spiritual professionals had put me down so much... The difference between the egotistical opinion of a human being who imagines himself to be the holder of the truth and the divine opinion is quite big!

I decided to wait and not say anything to anyone.
I didn't want to get carried away. If the request to write really came from the Archangels, they knew where to find me to give me a message again. This latent fear in me had developed a pervasive mind.
I was in constant analysis, dissecting everything.
I believed I wasn't a good person... Except that heaven doesn't care about limiting states of mind.
If the time for transformation has arrived, you must go with the flow!

The arrival of the Archangels marked the end of a cycle and the beginning of renewal. Stop destroying myself, stop hurting myself and stop molding myself to the expectations of others.

It was a cold night in December 2020. I watched one of my favorite series in its entirety until sleep took me away.

An old feeling, that of being sucked into a wormhole... When I landed, I recognized this green grass, this peaceful atmosphere, my mountain... I was back, 29 years later!

In front of me, 4 massive and imposing silhouettes were waiting for me. The colors emanating from them were blinding. It was a cameo of blue, white, green, bright gold...

I felt tiny in front of these powerful giants. The white figure spoke, not in words but in thoughts that passed from his mind to mine. I heard "You must write us letters, a life-changing teaching awaits you! We will help you!"

In an instant, it was over. The silhouettes became blurred, and I went back through the wormhole in the opposite direction. When I got back to my bed, I knew I wasn't hallucinating.

Younger, I could have put it down to my childhood imagination, although I never believed that! What happened to me at the time after Snoopy's death was real! What I had just experienced was direct contact with the Archangels!
Sleep was the only time my brain rested. They had entered the rift to get my attention. My first reaction is to check the time on my phone: 3.33am... Divine confirmation!

I got up and went to the window to get some fresh air, I needed a cigarette. A bad habit but it helped me to think about the message I'd just received.
Did I have the shoulders for this task? I had to stop asking myself too many questions...
I went back to bed and thanked God in a way I hadn't done for a long time...
During the week following the heavenly coming, I felt a wind of newness pushing me forward. I was overwhelmed with "flashes" of the big picture of my life. All those times I thought I was failing were just ways of doing things that weren't working so I began to understand where to go.

We tend to feel sorry for ourselves, for complicated relationships, for repetitive situations, for failures, for the passage of time... These paths that we imagine to be those of perdition are only the steppingstones that align our emotional intelligence with the supreme intelligence.

The main lines of life... I always believed that despite our free will, certain events are predetermined long before we are born. My clairvoyance were always to the point, "my voice" always telling me the important events of the past, present or future, depending on the person I was talking to. Gabriel will teach me the reasons for these outlines in his coaching…

Our free will is the learning ground that leads us to these intersections. No matter whether we take them or not, they will reappear in due course: to close or to transform. They are by no means fatalities or missed appointments!

They are points of light on the horizon that teach us to become free men and women. The Archangels' message gave me hope. I had taken so many muddy paths, followed so many risky methods... Now I had everything to gain! The only hesitation that remained was about the letters... I had no idea what to write to them. I couldn't believe that these four great powers were interested in me.

By following the rules and keeping everything to myself, I realized that I had never allowed anyone to know me. This was a chance to finally open to someone!

Words can twist many words and language can be a formidable weapon.With Michael, Gabriel, Raphael, Uriel or the friends of light from my childhood, I had the certainty that my confidences would be well kept and always used to my advantage.

One afternoon in January 2021, I settled down in the quiet. I had to start somewhere after all...

A hot coffee was waiting for me, some paper, a pen... I raised my cup high, toasting this beautiful adventure of the soul.

I was ready... to drink my first coffee with Archangels!

CHAPTER 6

Faith and Love...

"Faith is a guarantee of justice. Possessing it is a pledge of devotion to yourself."
Archangel Michael - 2021

You must fall many times to see the light... This is how I can sum up my two extraordinary night trips. I never thought I would return a second time to the peaceful plain of my childhood. I was still imbued with the atmosphere of this safe landscape and the beautiful colored auras emanating from the Archangels.

Each of them has a particular power of their own! Michael has the natural authority and solidity of the Father. His energy exposes us. With him, lying to ourselves is no longer possible because he exposes our deepest flaws. Gabriel carries the colossal energy of the Divine. To feel his aura is equivalent to returning to the womb, it is the regression towards the emergence of the possibilities that we repress. Raphael has global vision, he reads bodies, hearts and souls. His vibration regenerates and transforms to manifest other realities.

Uriel is the mature child, the one who knows but who contemplates the world with an ever-renewed happiness. Approaching him is to feel life in all its magic.

Together they form the love of God, the cohesion of forces that nothing can touch!

I was always logical and careful in my spiritual training. If a practice does not appeal to me, I prefer to refrain from any action whose consequences I don't know.

I may have missed opportunities to change my life earlier, but that's how it was, I think. With the Archangels, a new feeling was awakened: trust.

This time I wanted to go through with the experience. I had no idea where it was going to take me, but I believed!

I had only been given two instructions, to write letters and to receive a teaching that would help me. I saw myself as a student going back to school.
I was torn between excitement and the desire to do my best to do well. I knew that I would have my share of work to do.
My teachers were well known, but I knew nothing about their learning methods. Instinctively, my first letter was addressed to Gabriel. The quiet strength of his energy reminded me of the beautiful white angel of my youth, the one who had saved me from death...

I let myself be guided during the writing process, even though my ego told me that it was nonsense. Visually, it was a jumble of sentences and confessions without any logic.
Yet that blackened page marked my entry into faith and surrender. I felt invaded by new energies that gradually channeled me.
During my dreams, I received bits of information pushing me to talk to them more and more, to reveal feelings that I had never expressed. In return,

I got to know them and get an idea of the personality of each one.
I wrote... a lot... about myself, my life, my actions, my thoughts... I discovered the personalities of the four Archangels in a totally different light from the way they're portrayed.
It's a bit like hearing the gossip about celebrities and when you get to know them, you see that they're people like everyone else. What Michael, Gabriel, Raphael and Uriel have in common is that they love fairly, without judgement, while revealing different facets of love.

What I like most about them is that they don't impose anything. They suggest solutions but if a blockage arises, they take the problem from another angle to help solve it as best they can.
They are leaders, God gives them the freedom to act on how to follow his directives. However, they never take pride in their privileged position.
My correspondence with them took me out of the world of ego and into a healthy and constructive exchange. They put themselves within my reach

and they do it for each of us. Unlike the times I spent in society where I had to weigh every word to hope to be heard, here I felt good.

Regardless of any religious belief or personal conviction, faith is the cornerstone of any spiritual journey.

Opening one's conscience is not possible without deep faith. We resort to a form of faith that is rooted in despair or fear. Usually, we activate it when the point of no return is reached. When we experience a situation contrary to an instinct we have refused to follow and find ourselves on the brink.

What you think is faith becomes a lifeline that you cling to so that everything will work out. Newly discovered, it then leads to a spiral of waiting that destroys.

In short, this new bulwark makes us believe that we're in a process of trust, whereas inside we are in doubt and looking for answers. It is an open struggle between the ego that absolutely wants a form of result and the soul that knows the true goal.

Faith is a subtle mixture of love, trust, surrender and self-esteem.

Gabriel and Raphael were very instrumental in putting me on the path. I had to write letters to unseen recipients, to start putting this powerful energy into motion.

Some call it the law of non-resistance but I would say there is no hard and fast rule. My current vision of mountain-moving faith lies in the total acceptance of the present moment. Overcoming the ego and its trickery that keeps us from love.

Faith is the loving face of the ego. That decisive moment when the opening is finally made, and everything becomes clear. One finally understands that there is no need to fight. Surrendering becomes a strong act, it is the end of the tug of war between subtle perception and sometimes distorted certainty.

The treasure hunt ends, the gold flows freely, covering us with the greatest wealth of humanity... The surrender of control is the true promise of faith!

When this happened, my letters became less messy. The questions I was asking myself seemed trivial and I began to put events in my life into perspective. The Archangels don't like to leave their friends in the dark.

Through their guidance they took the time to unpack each of my questions. That's what I like about them, they don't improvise themselves as teachers, they are! They have the kindness to smile at you when you make discoveries that they already know.

This preparatory step began to strip me of what I imagined myself to be... Faith and love were now fully part of my life; the great teaching was approaching...

CHAPTER 7

Entering Magic

"Magic requires only one power: to be you!"
Archangel Raphael - 2021

Real magic is nothing like witchcraft!
A spell reflects an inner struggle and a will to control. It is driven by an unconscious desire to shape part of the world around us in our own image. This type of approach always carries with it traces of dissatisfaction, fear, lack or frustration…
There is never anything without something. Even when we are in the process of helping others, wanting to direct destiny at all costs by this process implies that the cause of the applicant is close to our heart. Unconsciously, a gap opens to bring repressed traumas to the surface. This kind of work is never done in complete neutrality, whatever one may say...

Even with the best protection in the world, the energies that accompany these procedures do not have only praiseworthy intentions. We then return to the circle of the eternal struggle of good against evil!

Divine Magic, on the other hand, is a hand extended from the powers of heaven. One chooses to accept it or not. Sometimes we don't even notice it because it is based on the unexpected in every detail. It's primarily a collaboration and a learning process, the purpose of which is to open our vision to each new fact.

With experience, alignment with the energy of manifestation becomes easier because we no longer feel the need to place our hopes on illusions.

The magic unfolds while respecting the rhythm of everyone. Apart from the promise of ever-changing knowledge and soul evolution, we have no certainty of what we are receiving. The magic adjusts so that it can be felt intensely.

When we begin to walk this path, the sky rolls out the red carpet so that the walk is smooth.

The best magician is the one who lives within us. He performs miracles as well as catastrophes... The personal abilities that we possess are always subject to a lack of objectivity. Let him who has never asked himself what he is good at, cast the first stone! Doubt in our powers is one of the factors that blocks the opening to other possibilities.

Except for the night when the Archangels spoke to me about the teaching I was to receive, they had not mentioned it again. In my letters, I asked questions which they answered, but this feeling of regression gave me the impression that I was at an impasse...
Of course, my analysis was different. It was thanks to them, and every step forward was helpful, but I was eager to get to the next level. Yet the progress of the last few months had been easy.

Everything I had tried so far had not been so fast, so I should not complain or give in to impatience. Besides, don't they say that discouragement comes when you are close to the goal? If I was honest with myself and questioned my heart, my greatest desire was to live serenely. I no longer wanted to feel guilty, beholden or obliged to please.

I felt like an outsider from this continual need for public recognition. Artificial lights are attractive, but once they are turned off, what is left?

I wanted more! What I desired was to wander happily through a life that was tailor-made for me.

A daily life of love and abundance in which I put all my energy into what I love.

It was no longer a question of running away from the obstacle. If it presented itself, it was surely to protect a part of me that was wrong or not ready.

I was tired of fighting invisible enemies when I was already out of the ring. No more injunctions, superstitions, fears, competition...

The world is dominated by the law of the strongest, and the magic that comes from it carries this root. It was time to deprogram myself from everything I thought I knew and reconnect with the Divine enchantment. I'd reached a point of no return. I had to leave behind the automatisms of adulthood to regain my childlike lightness...

To rediscover the pleasure of simple joys... Blowing on dandelions, going on rides at the fair, walking barefoot in the grass... All this accumulation of small spontaneities that didn't meet the criteria of fashion or beauty... Living, for better or for worse!
I wrote a long letter to the Archangels about these understandings. My words sounded like a heart cry, a confession of my despair at having gone so far without arriving anywhere...

Uriel himself came to answer me.
I was beginning to fall asleep when the sensation of leaving my body appeared. It was strange to be feeling so light. I was at home, everything seemed normal. I turned over and saw myself lying in bed, suddenly a halo of light filled the room.
Uriel was there, next to me, beaming as usual. The warm, soothing waves of his energy are like the sunshine of the seaside, when the sea air mixes with the ambient heat…
In his hands were a key and an hourglass. He held them out to me and said: *"The children of heaven are also the children of earth, they come down here to*

continue the Father's work,The root in the soil needs water and air to grow and take shape, it will face the elements, their calm, their anger,
The cycles will repeat themselves and come to an end, it will die ten times and rise again eleven, In the last hour before the day comes grace, Then the human will no longer be human but a face of eternity…"

Before disappearing, he added:
"Go back, the teaching will begin!"

Afterwards, "my voice" suggested that I be ready to take notes. I always had my mobile phone with me, I created a file to record everything when the time came...
The Archangels kept their promise, they gave me the keys to initiate changes in my life. The letters I had written to them earlier were just a warm-up.
I needed to experience some detachment before I could officially put things back in order.
I would no longer spread myself too thin. I was one of nature's many fruits and the magic of creation was at hand. It was up to me to activate it...

The teaching was simple and methodical, I would work first with Michael, then with Gabriel, then Raphael and finally Uriel.
I was at the foot of a great staircase and the exercises that were to be transmitted to me represented the steps of my evolution.

The distinct skills of each of the Archangels would help me to reach my Paradise, my reconstruction.
Earth, Water, Air and Fire...
Liberate, Feel, Heal, Enlighten...
That was the learning, the goal...
To bless the old to reunite the new...
I'm sharing this light coaching today so that you can make your life a source of miracles and magic!

PART 2

Basics of light coaching

CHAPTER 8

Introduction to light coaching

"Then His children will grow up in riddle but when they are ready, they will come to knowledge"
Archangel Uriel - 2021

Tradition and various experts list countless Archangels and angels. They're classified by fields of action and by hierarchy, but it would be a pity to limit them to names or functions.
This is very useful for identifying and recognizing them, but it should not be forgotten that on earth as in heaven, each one contributes to the building.

Let us have a loving thought for all the entities of light who work in conjunction with the forces of the Most High: ascended masters, guides, deceased, guardian angels...I share here an experience that literally transformed my life! For my part, I followed the instructions given to me to work with my friends of Light: Michael, Gabriel, Raphael and Uriel.

As some of the most recognized Archangelic figures, it may seem difficult to approach them. Yet all great leaders are wells of wisdom! It is belief that makes them inaccessible and puts barriers between us and them. Spiritual logic and the knowledge we have at our fingertips want us to follow a well-tuned mechanism in submitting our prayers by targeted problem.

I love the inhabitants of the celestial kingdom without making distinctions. They are all more radiant than each other but sometimes our human energy is not in tune with the luminous being we choose to call upon. This was the case for me for a long time. I tried to approach some of them for various problems, but it gave few results.

There was no mutual resonance! As in everyday life, if there is little or no affinity, the relationship will not go far. In spirituality, it is essential to be at ease in order to do good work. Luminous spiritual practice is based on collaboration.When the four powerful Divine emissaries came to me, I have no doubt that during our work together they mobilized additional forces of light to assist them. As I said, in the beginning I needed support and preparation...

During light coaching, the energy level goes through different stages.

To ensure evolutionary continuity, in rare cases, they may occasionally send other angels, guides or masters to help them, so as not to let an earthly misunderstanding take hold.

Their goal being the ascension of the person they help; they take over when the individual is ready to integrate the next teaching.

Fortunately, Michael, Gabriel, Raphael and Uriel have a large field of action allowing them to face all kinds of problems.

The human being is at one with nature. His origin is the light to which he will return when his work here is done. As we pass through, our body forms a very precise assemblage of each of the basic elements of creation:

- Earth: the body, matter, the root, the receptacle of the soul.
- Water: the fluids, the source of life, creation, intuition.
- Air: breath, sharing, cycles, movement.
- Fire: energy, radiation, action, concretization.

It's the symphony of our soul, its potential, its materialization.
Ether, considered as the fifth element, represents the finality, the quintessence. Michael, Gabriel, Raphael and Uriel are a concentrate of this perfection with the bonus of specific predispositions for each element. This only increases their power to help us with greater precision.

Light coaching is an initiation trip of the heart and soul. The goal is to awaken to yourself, to others, to circumstances, to lead you to wholeness in this life. Each step of this adventure aims to illuminate the shadows that obscure your life to transmute them into an inexhaustible source of personal abundance.

Engaging with and being guided by the Archangels will allow you to take charge of your life in complete autonomy, without depending desperately on external circumstances. It's the path to regained sovereignty, to inner reconciliation.

Writing is the foundation of each practical exercise. Do you remember the letters you used to send to Santa Claus when you were a child?
The correspondence with Michael, Gabriel, Raphael and Uriel is based on the same principle!
The light coaching is divided into four evolutionary stages and includes a total of 14 letters. This is what I call the different facets of light, from twilight to dawn. It starts with earth and ends with fire. Each Archangel corresponds to an element and deals with the main lifelines associated with it:

- First step/ Earth coaching (3 letters): the work on the Earth element with Michael is dedicated to the liberation of the body from family and external influences. Begin to understand our place and occupy our living space.

- Second step/ Water coaching (4 letters): the work on the Water element with Gabriel aims at intuition and its emergence to awaken the potentials of the soul in order to realign you to your life mission. The inexplicable intuition that guides you to manifestation.
- Third step/ Air coaching (5 letters): the work on the Air element with Raphael will lead you to the healing of the heart to reactivate your attraction force. Understand your life and transform your vibrational frequency to align with the energy of blessings.
- Fourth step/ Fire coaching (2 letters): working on the Fire element with Uriel represents rebirth and the sweeping away of the past. It is the radiance, the realization, the triumph after the effort. See the change and get concrete results, in agreement with oneself.

To ensure the best journey and not to burn out the steps, I advise to respect the initial work plan to write your letters. Start with Earth and climb the subtle spheres gradually with Water and Air to finish with Fire (which requires time and experience to be mastered properly). This allows for a gradual rise in consciousness and energy. Take time, give yourself time... Listening to yourself and your body is essential.

Wanting to move forward is good, without being too hasty is better!

Light coaching is accessible to all, beginners or advanced. Whatever your current level of spiritual evolution, you will receive what is right for you. In addition to consolidating what you already have, you will continue to learn.

Your letters are strictly personal! It's all about you.

If you mention other people in them, it will only be for the purpose of understanding for the upliftment and peace of your soul!

Once you are familiar with the energy of each Archangels, you can call upon them together or in pairs to guide you in your daily life. You cannot make a request to Archangels for someone else, even if it seems positive. Why? Because what you imagine to be good for a person you love may not be good in its reality. Such a claim wouldn't work because Archangels categorically refuse to take away anyone's free will.

However, they are not insensitive to the love we have for others. If they ever decide to support such a move, they will consider the situation of the person concerned first before your own desire for it.

They assume that everyone must have their own experiences and understandings.

It's an absolute condition of Divine Magic that the results are not as you want them but for the better!

This method of correspondence has absolutely nothing to do with automatic writing, which is a dangerous practice when one lacks discernment. With automatic writing, you have no control over your actions and your resonance. The entity responding to you may possess you momentarily, manipulate you and attempt to disrupt you.

Here you remain in balance from start to finish because the answers will not come in the moment, they come when you are ready. It may be hours, days or months, you are not the decision maker. Only God and his emissaries know the plan... The letters you write concern moments in your life that you already know that you experienced. You don't question the future; you only seek to make the best use of the past to improve the present and CREATE your future opportunities!

You are not waiting for answers either because you know they will come to you through signs, dreams, numbers, messages... Your soul will be helped to shine its light, but most of the work will come from YOU, only YOU. Once you have finished your letter, you put it in its envelope and leave it to our friends.

You simply ask if you can access the knowledge to transmute into light what no longer serves you. You place yourself in a position of welcome, ready to receive what is good for you.

There's no danger because you don't force any results! I share with you some stories from my life when I practiced light coaching. I've always considered that being a medium did not place me above others, I haven't been spared by tornadoes, so I've no lessons to give, only moments to share....

These pages are therefore an expression of my heart and my sincerity. I have a burning desire to help you lighten your burdens, so that your life may be beautiful and fulfilling. What seems insignificant can reveal the most incredible surprises...

I lived this journey of initiation intensely before the Archangels informed me that it was time to pass it on to you. I experienced what you will live, so I wanted a human and simple approach to share my knowledge with you.

I hope that in turn you will make wonderful discoveries alongside the Archangels. May the pain, fear and doubt leave you as you reveal to the world the incredible person you are!

CHAPTER 9

Protection

"Walking by His side, nothing can touch you..."
Archangel Michael - 2021

My mentor always told me: "It is faith that protects".
Any logical mind might wonder if the signs received in response to our letters are indeed from Archangels. For the reasons given in the previous chapter, the answer is YES!
However, doubt and fear are legitimate. When we open a spiritual connection, it is not excluded that third entities try to take a holiday in the human world. Some of these, very low in energy, try to play on imposture by pretending to be guides...
Even when you are a beginner, it is easy to recognize them.

Their presence quickly makes us uncomfortable, irritable, we may have headaches, suddenly get angry... Not everyone is a light guide! The true nature of these jokers is always revealed in the end.

A so-called "evil" or "demonic" entity will never help you to free yourself.

It is not interested in a liberation intention now, it is not in its initial vocation, nor in its evolutionary path. A low energy entity, seeing that it cannot enslave you in any way, will gain nothing by prolonging its presence at your side.

When we come across this type of presence in our lives, their role has a definite limit. They are merely the energetic spectrum of our buried terrors and manifest to confront our weaknesses. Everything has an end, only the light is eternal. If you are tired, worried or lack motivation, it is best to postpone your action to give yourself time to recover.

To boost your energy level, here is an affirmation to recite when the need arises:

"My dear Archangel Michael, outstanding strategist, Prince of the heavenly armies, thank you for cleansing

and transforming my energy of all patterns, attitudes, negative thoughts that don't belong to me. I walk in the truth and light of God; my goal is evolution and ever-renewed knowledge. I am guided and safe. So be it!"

The best motivation to work with the Archangels in complete safety is to keep as a goal to become a creator, an alchemist... In short, to turn your lead into gold!

Our energy bodies are well made. The physical and subtle layers form a first protective barrier.

Pollution of all kinds affects us all, without exception, and anyone who boasts that they have never been lying to you, no one is safe!

Fluctuating emotions are a natural state, put away the old superstitions from your head. Hazards, blockages and setbacks are part of our journey on earth. They are lessons and it is not always possible to avoid them, that would be to refuse a part of the incarnation contract.

Light and shadow are forced to live side by side. The shadow can only survive if it is given credibility. Even if you are not familiar with the world of angels, you will easily recognize the presence of Archangels at your side. Their vibration is unique: Michael liberates and balances, drawing out the old to prepare for the new.

Gabriel brings forth and strengthens, a veritable rain of light that soothes almost instantly.

Raphael transforms and heals, when he is there all physical and psychic fatigue disappears and Uriel animates and warms, his presence clarifies ideas and thoughts.

Your life no longer has the same color and flavor, you perceive it with more lightness. Moreover, they do things correctly by sending you confirming signs indicating the path to follow. They surround you and play down unfounded fears. Very often it's the mind that plays tricks so you must beware of it.

Once you have committed yourself to the path of recovered sovereignty, it will try to keep you in the old beliefs that no longer work. But as your link with the Archangels is based on knowledge, and by staying in this line of conduct, the shadow will not be interested in your desire to become the best version of yourself, and it will end up avoiding you like the plague.

Therefore, I insist that you write your letters in a place where you feel perfectly comfortable, and that there's not necessarily a need to follow a specific ceremony.

Any part of you that feels dissonant with a setting or practice will attract parasites. Working in a place you love and enjoy will already create a protective shield around you. Always have a representation of Archangels near you, this will strengthen your protection and help to establish direct contact. Trust them, as they believe in you very strongly.

You now understand that writing a letter in full consciousness isn't spiritualism!

Your request for help is addressed to an incorruptible energy source. By accepting to create this link, the power of Archangels is transmitted through you. That is why it would be very difficult for an impostor to survive such a high radiation! The faith that protects is the certainty that the dark forces have nothing to do with your path. Let us never forget that we are the sole authors of our happiness or misfortune.

The best protection we have is the strength of our convictions, and the kingdom of heaven is our unshakeable support...

CHAPTER 10

Writing and engaging in light

"Then from the interiorization will come the creation."

Archangel Gabriel - 2021

Man has always tried to use the ways of expression at his disposal to leave a trace throughout history. Archaeology and the study of ancient civilizations tell us much about the cultures that have shaped our world.

Many art forms, including writing, have helped to perpetuate the memory of these men and women of the past.

The Divine has been an inexhaustible source of inspiration for storytellers, thinkers and writers of all times. This transmission has ensured our knowledge of yesterday, today and tomorrow, showing us that many secrets are not revealed yet.

Words go, writings remain...
The great commitments of life are sealed in writing, engraving the idea and the action forever. This is how the light coaching of Archangels is built. Motivated by a strong will to commit to turning our past downfalls into resounding successes.
It was a major turning point in my spiritual life, putting me definitively on the path of faith and understanding after years of unhappiness, wandering and delusion. Today, I'm no longer afraid to do what I want to do because I have the strength and the belief to go through with my projects.

Words will always support our thoughts. Reciting a prayer can produce an uncertain result. When the mind wanders, the fervor decreases, and it is difficult to maintain a steady rhythm when one has 1000 thoughts in mind.
The letter, on the other hand, is an invisible thread that connects the past, the present and the future. It is a stable medium that the Archangels adore, they who are fond of knowledge...

Writing is a time for oneself, an intimate cocoon in which we are totally free. It is a space free of judgment! This activity, like painting or any other creative process, focuses the mind and opens the consciousness. The movement of the hand wielding the pen is peaceful, fluid, unconstrained...
The primitive instinct reconnects, thoughts are in order, the connection with the light grows and intensifies with each line...

Books are a part of my life. The beauty of words reflected the reality of feelings I couldn't express.
I dreamed, carried away by the enthusiasm of stories big and small.
Nowadays, the art of correspondence is slowly being lost. The letters of yesteryear have given way to tweets, private messages, text messages, posts, e-mails... We love each other, we communicate, we meet, we leave, we zap, we shape, we distort, dependent on a reality of pretense! Life through screens has gained disturbing ground, comfort has replaced effort. There's not a single minute of respite for our brains, which are constantly accumulating

information. The warmth of face-to-face dialogue is giving way to a virtual space of lament and open warfare. The world of light, although supporting technological progress, still resists the invader and those codes of behavior that drive us apart. It is a community that remains sensitive to the sincerity of a heart-to-heart conversation.

Choosing to ask for help from the higher planes is a sacred action. It requires patience, perseverance, faith and humility.

Putting your words on paper is a powerful symbol. You are agreeing to bridge the gap between the known and the unknown. Your concentration will channel the energy of the action; and if emotion ever comes into play, it will be structured because you are in the conscious mind. This means that you are absorbed in what you are writing and what your heart wants to say, the risk of external interference is almost zero.

Michael, Gabriel, Raphael, Uriel and all the other celestial entities are huge balls of love to be cherished. Writing to them is a deep and selfless expression of affection. You express yourself; you reveal yourself to them and in return you are aware that you are leaving them in charge of the blessings bestowed.

In life, when someone contacts you only when they need help, after a while your benevolence becomes saturated. You don't feel like answering the calls anymore, you feel that the person is abusing your time, your kindness and is using you with little consideration in return...

Without realizing it, we function in much the same way with the world of light. God, the masters, the angels, the guides... piles and piles of requested services pile up on their heavenly desks.... We rarely talk to them when things are going well, but when things are bad, we come to them... Do you see where I'm going with this?

As I got to know them and worked with them, I realized that they are not wish-fulfilment machines. They are not the good genies of the magic lamp! However, I can say that they help their fellow man in a wise way, looking after the welfare of all.

The writing gives way to a desire for KNOWLEDGE and EXCHANGE!

You create a closeness with them that is totally in line with your personality, your experience and who you really are. You gradually break out of the mold of collective belief...

Light coaching is as simple as that: accept to be guided in complete confidence. It's a 50/50 deal where everyone works in harmony with love and respect. In one of my first letters, I asked them why my prayers were not always answered. In one of my dreams, the four of them answered me in a very sincere way:

"You had no time for yourself or for us, how did you expect us to give you time in return?"

This answer was obvious, and they were so right.... They had heard me perfectly, except that I was not willing to listen to them! These refined, cultured, humorous people deserved better than a ready-made prayer recited without conviction! They deserved better than someone who turned his back on them for years while they were still around. They deserved love, real love, and so do I... Once again, they were the voice of wisdom.

Starting a written correspondence with the Archangels means stopping hiding.

With them, you can allow yourself to reveal your faults, your mistakes, your little quirks, your opinions, your moments of weakness, your fears, your sorrows, your joys, and ask them to help you in whatever serves your highest good.

The great principles of positive spirituality teach us that this is not a good thing. They are right to say that stirring up the negative is harmful. However, extreme interiorization is not a solution either. It means burying or denying whole parts of life...

To free yourself, there is this method which consists of writing a letter and burning it. You can't even imagine the energetic violence of the act!

You will see it in the part dedicated to Uriel: fire, before purifying, destroys... Piling up your emotions on a sheet of paper and then turning it into ashes... it's like receiving a backlash! It's the disguised way of keeping the fire of unhealed feelings alive.

I've been there, so many times I can't count them... I was temporarily appeased until the harmful and destructive feelings came back tenfold.

In the end, isn't it a lasting peace that we are looking for? Stop beating yourself up and imagining that there is an eternal price to pay for accepting to be you!

You have found excellent people to talk to, for that is what the Archangels are looking for: authenticity. The more they get to know you, the more they will reveal themselves in return!

EXCHANGE and KNOWLEDGE, that is how they will bless you... so that in the future you form the most luminous of teams!

CHAPTER 11

How do you formulate your letters?

"Express the desire of your heart and we will hear it"
Archangel Raphael – 2021

Archangelic light coaching teaches many lessons. One of them is to unlearn and deprogram the known in order to take part in your own life.

No longer are we talking about being extras or stealthy appearances on the stage of your destiny, but about returning to being in the foreground. In spirituality, apart from certain limits to be fixed concerning certain practices, there is no exact science.

Undergoing a ritual that does not resonate deeply with your consciousness and intentions will not lead to any results. If, for example, you don't like incense, candles, crystals or anything else, don't impose a practice on yourself that makes you uncomfortable.

The goal is to reconnect with your personal universe! It is important to write in a setting that you like, in which you feel good. You should answer the call of the writing. It doesn't matter what day, time or specific time of the month it is. If you want to set up a rhythm of work, do it!

Otherwise, just let it happen... You can write as many letters as you like, of any length. You can talk about absolutely everything without restriction, the Archangels are there to listen to you.

You may also feel the need to take a break to integrate certain stages of the teaching, know that this is normal so take all the time you need to do so. Instinctively, as you become more aware, you will know exactly when the next exercise is best.

You must not block anything, try not to be in the mind. Spirituality is not a race for results, it is your own progress that matters. Correspondence with Archangels will teach you to follow the cycle of your body and your consciousness.

In my case, I like to write in the evening and at night, when my brain disconnects from the hustle and bustle of the day. I have never been attracted to all the gimmicks that tend to make a process seem more efficient. Now I do things as I feel them.

I prefer simplicity so, for my letters, I take a sheet of paper, a pen and the St. John Church Archangels.
I may also write on my computer if I have an urgent message for them. Some nights, if I am tired, I don't force myself to write at all costs.
I assume that the next day will have something to teach me, and that there will always be time to discuss it with our light friends.

Be creative, don't become a spiritual slave!
Do everything you want and don't limit yourself! You will find that discipline will come more easily if you experience it this way. Feel in tune with your environment and your personality, you don't need more.
The letters you write during the light coaching will include some wording guidelines. This corresponds to the area of life that will be worked on with each Archangel. These are the key steps that will trigger

the transformation processes. As far as content and form are concerned, you are free to write as you wish. Indeed, you will be working to create a link between you and Heaven.

Forget about not being a seasoned writer, the Archangels do not care. It's not the everyday mask they want to see, they always have an eye on you, so they know everything. What they are interested in is what you are, without artifice or manners!

You are not in the middle of a group that you want to make a good impression on! Come as you are, natural, without complexes! That's what makes you so beautiful and unique at the same time.

Whether you write ten lines or fifteen pages, that's fine! The important thing to remember is that we all start somewhere, and it takes a lot of wrong answers to get to the right one. Decompress and let go of the guilt, enjoy yourself without worrying about convention.

Another crucial point will be the way you address the Archangels. We have been taught all our lives that they are superior and that you almost must show a white coat to talk to them. Barriers, more barriers...

Yes, it's true, they have an extremely high vibration! Besides, it would be impossible for our human constitution to bear an energy load like theirs.

We would either end up seriously ill or completely mad! Moreover, it is a big kick in the ass for intolerant people who impose and demand ideal purity criteria to be a "good" person.

Can you imagine what it would mean to go from standard human radiation to divine radiation in an instant? It would be like being struck by lightning!

Let's start with this simple fact: Human = Life on Earth = here to learn and, if you'll pardon the expression, to take a dump sometimes!

Keep it simple, it's your best asset! Nothing prevents you from being friends with the Archangels or other entities of light.

You can completely understand the closeness that you can have with your guides, your deceased, God? Yes, because they are beings that you love.

We are all family, so don't stop at a rank or hierarchy.

You can totally expand your network of divine

friends! The energy of the Archangels will simply adapt to yours and you will gradually integrate theirs to raise your consciousness. If in your letters you want to be formal and conventional, do so!

Afterwards, if you prefer to speak more familiarly, no one will blame you, especially not them!
Start your letter with "Dear Archangel Gabriel", "Dear Michael", "My friend Raphael" ... It doesn't matter, if it brings out that little creative spark that characterizes you.
The end of your letter should also be in line with your beliefs. If you like to say "Thank you, Amen, so be it, Namaste etc." don't change anything.
Keep that habit that you like instead of replacing it with another that will not resonate with your belief.
Your spiritual contact with the Archangels is like a blank canvas. From the preparatory drawing to the final touch, you apply yourself to create a work that pleases you and makes you proud.

To help you visualize, I give you an example of how I formulate my own letters.

We'll say I'm working on the Divine Masculine exercise with Michael:

From:

Born:

"My dear Archangel Michael,

I am writing to you today to ask for help and understanding about my Divine Masculine in order to harmonize my sacred Earth. I therefore submit to you a list of all the male persons I can remember who have passed through my life:

- D.M (father)

- A.E (classmate)

- L.O (ex-boyfriend)

Thank you for using your liberating and purifying force to harmonize my Sacred Masculine and transmute all energetic residues that are now useless to me into pure love light. For my good and that of the people mentioned. I thank you from the bottom of my heart for your support in my evolutionary process. I have full confidence in the revelations and solutions that you will place on my path. Thank you, thank you, thank you! I love you!"

Explained in a theoretical way, I grant you that the process may seem complicated or daunting. In practice, you can see that there is nothing difficult about it. Now that you have the cards in your hand, it is up to you to arrange your deck as you wish. Once you have written your letters, you must ask yourself what you are going to do with them.

Personally, I took five large envelopes. Four of them have the name of the Archangel to whom the letter is addressed. I like colors so I wrote each name in the tone that corresponds to the field of action of each one:

- Blue for Michael
- Gold for Gabriel
- Green for Raphael
- Red for Uriel

The fifth envelope is for the "collective" letters. When I need a deeper understanding and do not yet know which of the four Archangels can help me.

I chose purple instinctively. This has nothing to do with it being the spiritual color by excellence but

because I like it and it calms me. I keep the letters in a place known only to myself.
Do I ever read them again? Never!
They're linked to a specific moment or question. Once they are in the envelope, I consider the situation resolved and part of the past.

My way of doing things is given as an example to serve as a basis, but it may not be suitable for you. Personalize and adapt the coaching to what you think will work for you. You may want to bury your letters, keep them, send them, throw bottles into the sea...
There are so many possibilities, act according to your mood!
Be the child with the mischievous eyes. The one whose loud laughter echoes off the walls of the room.
Have fun believing that anything is possible...

CHAPTER 12

Gratitude

"When we support you, we expect nothing more than the spontaneity you keep in your heart!"
Archangel Uriel - 2021

Love, faith and gratitude are the highest forms of natural protection that exist. These pure emotions are the pillars of the angelic world and naturally repel anything that does not vibrate at the same level. Gratitude is a very important part of working with the Archangels. It is a subject that has been seen many times, but it is always good to talk about it.

Prayer, law of attraction or spirituality in general always includes gratitude in its action protocols. Giving thanks in the belief that you have already received, a sure thing to rely on. But... I don't want to question the foundations of methods that have proven themselves for some of us. Nevertheless, I am thinking of those for whom the manifestation is slow to arrive and who give in to discouragement. Again, I emphasize that these people are not weak, impure, unlucky or anything negative. They are human and thankfully so!

Want to know the secret of gratitude?
Stop conditioning yourself into automatic thanks! Although it tends to get lost, most of us know the codes of society and politeness. We're programmed from childhood to say "Hello", "Goodbye", "Please" and "Thank you". These words and expressions are an integral part of our vocabulary. They are used to communicate in everyday life, to get to know each other, to access needs... "Thank you", which is the verbalization of gratitude, is used so often in one's life that it loses its strength.

Naturally, it is this word that is expressed to end a request and put gratitude into action... Unfortunately, between theory and practice, there's a gap the size of the Grand Canyon among the two! In life, every word you say must come from your heart and soul. I really understood the magic and impact this word could have on people and things when I stopped saying it automatically.

Saying thank you out of politeness or obligation is anything but gratitude! As a result, I was moving away from the desired effect...

I'll take a concrete example: I often went to shops and met employees who were far from being at their best. Being in constant contact with customers can be difficult and having worked in retail I know that this kind of work can put nerves on edge. Even when an employee is very unpleasant, I always say "thank you, have a nice day".

Socially, this is the way to go. The other person's reaction to me is their own and I don't have to take it personally. Only, when I started practicing Archangel Light Coaching, the question of gratitude came up, so I observed my daily life.

Let's go back to our unpleasant employee. Finally, if I put aside politeness, why did I thank him? For receiving his contempt in the face! I thought I was being nice or brightening his day, until I realized I

was thanking him for being treated like a nobody. Existence is a constant exchange of energy.
With my formal thank you, I was encouraging the person in their arrogant attitude, and I was only putting myself down. We agree that presented in this way there is an imbalance...Spiritual gratitude is the same!

If you give thanks for an intention that is contrary to your intuition, it is forced gratitude that reassures you. You are in doubt, or you don't "feel it" but you consider that you have done the right thing... Because it had to be done! How can you give thanks for a blessing received when your heart is not convinced?
Unintentionally, you maintain this doubt and give it power over you. Incidentally, you are busy giving a few more shovelfuls that only make the canyon bigger...

Gratitude comes from bliss and listening. Since I've learned to trust myself, I wonder at little things I wouldn't have noticed before. It makes me feel good and my heart always feels happy. I meet a lot of nice people and the words I say vibrate with my state of mind. Materially, wonderful synchronicities keep pushing me towards happiness.

Like "I love you", "Thank you" is a precious word that must come from within. It must resonate from within, explode the decibels...

It must be spontaneous and in total accord with the simple joy of the heart.

The second case that can cause a block in the exercise of gratitude is obligation. You can easily visualize this image of a donkey struggling to move forward. To make him go where you want him to go, you wave a carrot under his nose... At the sight of such a beautiful reward, the donkey complies without flinching!

Some spiritual principles have no qualms about using the same device. We put on the costume of the donkey that wants its carrot... We must preserve the "virtuous circle" of waiting for a brilliant manifestation. To maintain the circle, we are advised to meditate, to make sure we have only positive thoughts 24 hours a day, to pray... So many recommendations, so much effort to make, difficult to apply in the long term while keeping the beautiful motivation of the beginning!

Some people don't want to impose constraints on themselves, they are not ready for that!
They may simply need to let life takes them... Because practicing gratitude under the conditions I have just described causes an increase in stress and feeds the belief that we are not doing things right. One anxiety replaces another and brings an approximate or even non-existent result...
Forgive my frankness, but do you see that fucking sword of Damocles hanging over your head? This isn't the kind of leap of faith that the Universe or the Divine Kingdom requires!

I found myself in a bind for a long time because of this type of imperative. When I asked for advice, I always got the answer "Yes, but you didn't put enough into it". Wait a minute, I'm not a magician pulling rabbits out of my hat! Instead of an accusation disguised as an assertion I would have much preferred an explanation. The greatest ills call for the greatest remedies! I took advantage of my correspondence with the Archangels to ask them what they thought was the best way to express my gratitude.

Here is the answer Uriel gave me: *"Make yourself happy!"*

Simple but effective! And blatantly obvious to boot! This revelation made me want to ask myself a simple question.

Had meditating, fasting, paying attention to my thoughts made me happy? For me, it's a big NO!

At least not under these conditions...

I felt as if I had received an additional punishment... On top of the ones, I already inflicted on myself. The most beautiful reward for the Archangels is to see their proteges happy.

I then understood that seeing me smile and make myself happy was the most beautiful sign of gratitude I could give them. Doing good to me means doing good to them, we are really moving forward together in this perspective. I've gradually changed my way of life. I have a childlike joy in having bouquets of flowers at home, when I buy them, I always think of my bright friends. Moreover, my florist often gives me beautiful lilies to complete my floral arrangements... It is not difficult to guess that Gabriel is behind the divine idea that inspires this special attention to me!

I love buying gifts for my loved ones, it's one of the moments in life that makes me very happy.

Make nice packages, writing little cards that the person will read again one day... Participating in the creation of a memory, in some way.

I'm tired of over-consuming so I chose to buy just one good quality piece of clothing every month. Now I don't have a fashionable dressing room, I have a treasure chest that suits me and makes me smile.

I love the simple moments spent in the company of my dogs and my loved ones... Not once do I feel punished, my joy is natural! I am happy, I smile, my heart sings... On the Archangel side I feel the same energy. Your gratitude that blesses is in what animates you and makes you happy, so the floodgates open to prepare you for the good surprises of your destiny.

CHAPTER 13

Simplicity and power

"What He gives you, accept it with humility, share it with a generosity devoid of pride..."
Archangel Michael - 2021

Any spiritual journey must be based on a search for truth! Seeing oneself invested with new capacities is exhilarating, suddenly one feels special. This impression of standing out from the crowd gives you wings; you are tempted to see yourself differently. You know that deep conviction that you have that little extra something that others don't see, don't have.

At the beginning, the secret is jealously guarded, the time it takes to quench this thirst for learning which becomes more and more invasive. Little by little, confidence is established and if it is good to keep a touch of humility, the personality can quickly take an uncertain and dangerous path: that of POWER!

The very definition of power is to have POSSIBILITY. When exercised in this way, power is healthy because it means drawing on your own inner reserves to carry out a project.

It also means having the courage to admit your shortcomings, to say loudly and clearly that "I don't know" which puts you in a weak position according to the person you are talking to. Overall, you make do with your initial strengths and weaknesses.

But power, in its other meaning, is to HAVE THE RIGHT. And here we must be careful not to enter a dark forest.

It is common to make the mistake of thinking that being spiritual invests us with mission and that we can have the right, or even grant ourselves the right, to intervene in the lives of others without causing problems. Whatever the level of elevation, no one is God!

Why not care about the other person's emotions when compassion and humility are more rewarding. On the contrary, to be humble enough to consider with equality the person to whom one extends a

hand demonstrates a genuine nobility of soul. Every man on this earth is only passing through.
A social, intellectual or spiritual condition will not exempt us from this finality that awaits us all, this great journey that transforms matter into a trail of powder....

Simplicity, accessibility and understanding are the foundations of a healthy and beneficial spirituality. Accepting that you are only passing through the other person's life and helping them as best you can while enriching yourself with an incredible human story. The world of light does not deprive us of our free will, so what man could claim to do so? To accumulate knowledge, understanding and to misuse it for the purpose of gaining external recognition is a recipe for failure!
One does not develop oneself and one does not help others in order to take pride in oneself or to tell imaginary stories!
Practicing spirituality, whether personally or professionally, does not grant a supreme right of life or death over others. Wielding higher forces is never

without consequences. It is folly to believe that one can muzzle the course of destiny or pronounce firm and definitive verdicts... This is to misunderstand heaven and its mysteries!

Spiritual power should not be used to put a layer of varnish on one's problems in order to occupy the position of a guru in the eyes of others.
It is generally known how this kind of experience ends...
Rising in consciousness is a lifelong learning process. It is the contract of trust that helps you to get up after every fall. It is the essence of power; it is accepting mistakes and sometimes even ignorance.

Your only baggage is the certainty that what you have learned will be useful to you later. The only responsibility we have is strictly individual. In our relationships with others, we must only accept the idea of being an occasional guide for them at a key moment in their lives.
So, to embark on the path of spirituality out of egotism, a need for domination or a pure inferiority

complex is an experience that will be fraught with consequences... I am not convinced that it is worth the effort.

At one point or another, those who practice excessive power will be called to order... Keeping it simple means feeling good about yourself without taking advantage of superiority over others.

We can reach high degrees of wisdom, but we must not lose sight of the fact that the advisors are not the payers. The other never belongs to us, he teaches us, he completes us!

You are about to enter the purely practical part of the teaching that the Archangels have given me.

A great majority of the work process includes others, but not once will it be about power over them. Rather, it will be about awakening and expanding your own possibilities. You will be entering a sphere where freedom prevails, and simplicity is the prerequisite for taking full advantage of your cooperation with Michael, Gabriel, Raphael and Uriel. Together you will begin the most wonderful journey, guiding you towards the light of your heart.

PART 3

The Archangels' light coaching, welcome to your new self

CHAPTER 14

Journey to the heart of the self

Michael - God-like

"I remember the first time I saw a representation of Archangel Michael. I must have been 5 or 6 years old. On Sundays, my parents often took my sisters and I to the Abbey of Saint-Michel de Frigolet, a little paradise located in the mountains of Tarascon.

I loved the calm and quietness that emanated from this place where you could feed the animals and picnic in the shade of the pine trees. There, time stands still, life flows peacefully to the rhythm of nature and the sound of bells. The church, which forms the heart of the Abbey, was a must for our visit.

At the entrance, a huge statue of St. Peter made of olive wood guards the home of the prince. The atmosphere of the place encourages silence, only the sound of footsteps disturbs the rest that suddenly invades the soul. It is then that he appears, tall and strong, enthroned majestically on his pedestal. The haughty posture in which he has been immortalized commands respect and dazzles my childish eyes. He's the power against which no dark force can fight… Michael... Nestled in the heights is his sanctuary…

A few kilometers away, on the ground, the Tarasque, the legendary demon of Provence, rests in its place... It's a wonderful paradox to confront the power of heaven with the terror of men…"

The Earth - Understand, Feel, Liberate

"I'll make you a flourishing land…"
Archangel Michael - 2021

The Earth, this beautiful planet on which we live, is the element that makes up matter. The fruit of divine creation, the earth, through the stages of its

formation, represents the perfect outcome of evolutionary cycles. Its heart carries the memory of each of the elements (air, fire, water) that have participated in the elaboration of its present form.
It perfectly illustrates the concept of birth, death and resilience. Strength, solidity and density are the key words that describe it. Indeed, our physical body is an extension of this earth, one of the animate and conscious parts that help perpetuate creation. The first stage of light coaching begins here.

The Earth has taken billions of years to become the place we now call home. Naturally, it underwent its various mutations before stabilizing its final structure. Each human being is a small planet in the making, the union of a body and a divine soul.
A soil conducive to the cultivation of the most beautiful seeds... But before the flourishing harvest, a period of fallow land is essential. The land must be cleared and ploughed before it can be sown...
The actual size of the body does not matter... The land is vast and even with the best will in the world, getting rid of sprouted seeds, stubborn roots and

weeds can become a real obstacle course. This is a good thing, because the mission will be supervised by a professional in the field: Michael!

When the Archangels told me that I was ready to be taught by them, I was a little apprehensive about the moment when I would have to work with Michael. I think that of all the angelic figures, he impressed me the most from a very young age! Michael always had a special place at home. A statue of him stood proudly on the family sideboard. You could say that I grew up with him...

Before I started, I thought of him as a stern old professor, whose reputation and knowledge are unquestionable... I was not so much mistaken. If there was a ranking of the most beloved Archangels, I would have no doubt that he would be at the top of the podium.

A true figurehead of absolute triumph over the forces of evil, the areas of action for which Michael is most sought after are undoubtedly the protection and cleansing of negative energies.

He is the reassuring power that can be relied upon in inextricable situations. My esoteric and spiritual journey has brought me across people who have anchored in my mind that this prestigious divine emissary could never help a person like me.

He was not just anyone, his great moral strength could only serve the spiritual elite and the righteous... Afterwards, it's not necessarily possible to change the narrow vision of some people, so let's strip ourselves of judgments that don't help us.

This blatant human distinction between right and wrong has kept me away from Michael for years. So many people with pseudo-superpowers judged me and condemned me to the worst, I feared a harsh verdict from the Prince of Armies. In any case, if he and I were destined to work together for some time, my apprehension would not help me move forward.

My light coaching was to begin in openness, not fear! It was obvious that I didn't know Michael very well as my misgivings were quickly dispelled.

He came to me in a dream. He was huge and motionless; his ethereal beauty touched my heart. I

was reassured by his presence and when he pointed his sword above my head, everything started to swirl around me at a crazy speed.
I suddenly sat up in bed, still stunned by this unexpected visit. All my fears had disappeared, his sword had seemingly sucked them away. From that moment on, I was certain that Michael could come to meet anyone who asked him. Instead of relying on superior knowledge, I realized that I had been relying on biased truths that belonged only to the holder…

"I am not a bulwark but a bridge!"

This was the phrase I heard when I woke up and everything became clear!
Until now, when I had tried to pray to Michael, I had always followed a strict protocol of invoking him to ward off and cast out the demons around me.
In fact, when you think about it, we spend our lives fighting visible and invisible 'enemies'. For those who believe in and use him, Michael is the lifeline

that makes things right with the snap of a finger. "I am not a bulwark but a bridge" a few words that mean so much...

The concepts of victory/defeat are very human notions. A way of intellectualizing what is beyond us so that it can be understood by as many people as possible. Michael's energy is used as a shield to escape the important lessons of life (the demons).

To use a very unpoetic metaphor, shit is hidden under the carpet. Visually it looks clean, but the stench is persistent!

Good and evil are concepts subject to morality and personal interpretation.

Spending time fighting makes us alive and gives us a reason to exist, to demonstrate our individuality. I am no exception as I have followed the herd for a long time. My lifestyle and limiting beliefs got me into a crusade that distracted me from the real issue. All these demons, spells and curses were giving me a good excuse to not be the person I wanted to be.

The first confrontation between light and shadow starts in childhood. Later, our development only accentuates our rebellions.

The repetitive and outdated arguments that explained my failures were only invisible barriers of the ego. It is with this mindset that we call on Michael, hiding behind his warrior power in the hope that he will be the bulwark between us and what we don't want to see.
If I wanted to start my life again with a clean slate, I had to face up to all my experiences, unconditionally and without detours to replace the bulwark with the bridge!

Michael is the leader of the heavenly armies.
A brilliant military man and strategist, his brief message gave me the tone of what his teaching was going to be: to take the elements from the beginning and in order. Stop submitting isolated situations to him without having a global view of the battlefield. To act effectively, he needs a clear plan of action.

My body and consciousness being an extension of the earth, I had to dive into the underground galleries of the EGO to take stock. This meant going through my flaws. More than once I had done this

and it had been used against me, except that now my case had been classified in high places.
Was I ready to meet my demons? Time would tell...
Rigor and discernment are the order of the day with Michael. He never gives up, so he expects the same mindset from those he helps.
Before discovering the rest of the program, I took the time to look at the existing representations of him. Of course, the general aspect that jumps out is his absolute triumph over the devil, but beyond that let's focus on the expression on his face.
And there, we discover him calm, serene, sure of his actions and his choices... He shows no signs of inner or outer conflict...
The image of the one who has nothing to lose nor to prove since he already has everything! The demon, on the other hand, is agitated and struggles despite the domination of the prince... What if the evil one is inside us but not in the form we imagine?
What if this rebellious body that wriggles under the sword is only the face of our ego, the restlessness that inhabits us... The proud doubt that tries to annihilate the unshakable confidence... The real

fight between God and the Devil, our divine part against our earthly part!
The first part of my correspondence with Michael was to follow a precise plan to bring order to the minefield. To learn soon the steps to prepare the future harmony between my promised land (my body, my present, my life) and the Divine (my mission).

Back to origins...

"The Earth is home to a multitude of fates and lessons. To perform the individual miracle is to participate in the collective miracle..."
Archangel Michael – 2021

The family is the starting point of any earthly incarnation. The union of two people creates the future carnal envelope that will serve as our receptacle for life.
On the subtle level, the choice of the soul concerning the family unit that it will integrate is never the fruit

of chance. The place in the siblings, the links that will unite us to our loved ones... Everything is divinely orchestrated to provide the soul with the evolutionary lessons it will need. The beginning of all human relationships starts here!

Our ancestry represents a part of the light and shadow aspect present in each of us. It gives an indication of our future constructions and deconstructions. Certain links will be favorable to us, they will develop love, trust... While others will develop rejection, anger, resentment...

We carry within us our individuality; this is the initial programming inscribed in the life path. Fragments of parents and ancestors are also present, and we are sometimes unaware of their existence. Nevertheless, whatever we are led to believe, we do not belong to our relatives. We are just passing through. We can love them with all our heart, resent them, hate them, ignore them... but on the great chessboard of life, each piece is in its place.

Different and yet similar... Some will experience a heavy family history that will leave many scars, while others will thrive in a protective cocoon of love. But this isn't a basic criterion that will define everyone's destiny; starting out with a certain advantage does not guarantee a life path as light as a feather. No matter where you come from, what you are...

These first joys and wounds are only rites of passage necessary for understanding. Everyone feels inhabited by ghosts one day or another.

Family lines are like a spider's web. The cells, the DNA, are the threads that make it up. This tangle of destinies and genetic characteristics forms the beginning of everything that represents us. The multiple stages of the formation of the Earth in the universe!

Here begins the action plan of the light coaching.

As we know, Michael is not a bulwark, and it is not healthy to hide or deny our origins. It is obvious that the first teaching is in this area…

The family that my soul chose to integrate into has always been relatively disunited.

Whether it was my father's or my mother's side! My grandparents were indifferent to the presence of their granddaughters.
I don't remember any complicity with them. My maternal grandparents didn’t want to be called grandfather or grandmother. My father's parents worshipped my older sister... My little sister and I didn't even exist in their eyes.
My father managed to be absent, and when he was there, he terrified me. He was cold, angry, unloving... My mother, on the other hand, looked after us and the house, she was still young when her health problems hit her... We needed to be quiet so as not to fatigue her... The very structure of the core was defective...

There was much injustice at home and little joy. Family outings were like an obstacle course, there was no room for spontaneity. We never went on holiday; we didn't go to restaurants... It was a quasi-monastic daily life where the only rule was to obey, undergo and remain silent. Simple pleasures were not allowed to pass through the door, and if they did, fate would automatically chase them away. Despite the presence of my brilliant friends at that time, I still remember the tarnished joys and the perpetual boredom...

Deep inside I was seething, like a bull ready to charge at the sight of the red flag. My only two rebellions as a child earned me severe corrections from my father that I will not forget... From that moment on, I chose to keep quiet and watch the family debacle in silence...

The first stones of my bulwark were built on anger and a feeling of powerlessness!

I didn't see my family as a potential lesson but as a divine punishment to be atoned for. I would add to that a touch of egotism because I often asked myself with annoyance why I had ended up there... I saw myself as the only pawn on the chessboard against the rest of the board...

A flash of insight came to me on this subject after Michael's visit. A surge of anger, of that dull rage that led to problems of communication and self-esteem...

The memory of certain moments in my life awakened the monster lurking deep in its cave. I was not only carrying my revolt, but I was also the revolt!
Bringing back those memories that I had locked up in the depths of my soul made me numb. But Heaven never admits defeat and knows how to set its forces in motion long before the body acts.
My first work with Michael was going to be very challenging!
I had no one to blame because the realization came from me, from this truth that I had long denied. I felt as if the sense of security that I had felt over the last few months was just an illusion. I was afraid I wouldn't make it... Except that God knows all hearts and knows how his messengers should approach the obstacle to overcome it.

I buried these sorrows and feeling them resurface made me angry. Old patterns die hard. I started to ruminate the old way again, like "Every time I try to get out of it, something gets in my way!". Luckily Michael is not one to get discouraged... He had knowledge to pass on to me, and he used the right means to get me back on track.

One morning I was tidying up and cleaning my library. My books are arranged by size because I am obsessed with aligned stacks. On this day, one of the books on the shelf was slightly out of line with the others. Sacrilege!

And I remember very well not putting it back in that order. I was curious to see which book it was Volume 20 of Les Rougon-Macquart: Docteur Pascal. I could swear I didn't touch it!

Instinctively, I took it to leaf through it. I have a little ritual of closing my eyes and turning the pages until I feel I must stop. An old childhood habit that has stuck...

The paragraph I was guided is the one where Clotilde Saccard, niece of Doctor Pascal, intrigued by an ever-locked cupboard in her uncle's office, tries to find out what's in it. Inside are the Doctor's studies on his genealogy... Patient and painstaking work on each member of his family to try to determine how the scales of heredity tip...

Okay Michael, I get the message!
He used one of my favorite novels to gently lead me into working through my first failure.
Family is the first school of life. The study of soul ties and transgenerational wounds teaches that we carry not only our unfinished missions, but also those of our loved ones. Transfers and knots are made, drawing us into a system of thought that leads us to believe that our inheritances are fatalities that cannot be undone.
Doctor Pascal... it makes senses! This emblematic character spent his life trying to reconstitute his origins, dissecting the personality of each family member, even though he himself had hereditary flaws… As the perfect leader of naturalism, Emile Zola has put down on paper the most beautiful transgenerational fresco in literature.
The Rougons, the Macquarts... the "prestigious" branch and the "waste" of the lineage.
Those whose destiny seems written in advance because the incarnation has decided on a family name. They can fight, despise, accuse and deny each other... but nothing takes away the link and the

place of each on the chessboard! I understood that I could be afraid and use silence as a shield, I am a full member of my family!

Life predisposes us to certain unpleasant legacies, to unfounded comparisons that stick to us.

We are part of this whole even though wanting to escape it, to break free, to think we are different... We become braced in incomprehension and resentment. What if we put aside for a moment the causes and their consequences to concentrate on the strengths that our lineages transmit to us?

Let us abandon the need to prove something and rediscover the desire to learn from those whose blood and flesh we share...

Coaching No. 1 – 1st Letter

Cleansing and releasing family roots

"Your roots are the origin of uniqueness..."
Archangel Michael - 2021

The beauty of spiritual understandings is that one can return to a piece of information indefinitely and always find treasures. Knowledge is always available to those who are not closed.

This first letter of light coaching is about unearthing buried family memories. Misunderstandings, traumas, misinterpretations, values...

Everything that was done to us or instilled in us as children and that caused major developmental flaws. These are the demons that take on the face of filial love, baggage that is far too heavy to be left behind. In short, release the old to create a space for renewal. Every family bond has its importance. Our missions towards each other are temporarily postponed according to our understanding. This release exercise does not consider distance, being near or far from your family does not change the purpose of the process.

It is the emotion of the memory that is crucial and will trigger Michael's transmutation energy. The goal is to raise your vibration and that of the people involved.

First, I drew a diagram of a tree. I focused on Michael to anchor his energy and remind him who my loved ones are, even if he already knows them. At the bottom, I wrote my name, and then I gradually moved up the "branches" by mentioning the people in my family.

I advise to start with the close family (parents, brothers, sisters...). They form the core, the center of the earth, the direct lineage. End with the family members with whom there is the least interaction. This is the secondary lineage.

The diagram should be free form. When you look at it, it reminds you of the inverted triangle, symbol of the earth.

The names you write will only be connected by a line, so you don't put anyone in a box. Intention and the mind are not the only factors for success in spirituality.
Symbolism is also very important because it is what immediately catches the eye. Through the eye, the subconscious mind records images which it then stores in memory.
Most wounds, disagreements, misunderstandings and family traumas lead to a feeling of confinement. The aim is to transmute distended bonds into light. You free yourself and the other person from toxic and negative roots.
They are independent personalities!

Family members involved:

- Parents, grandparents, brothers, sisters…

- Uncles, aunts, cousins, stepparents, step-brothers, step-sisters…

This is the general idea of your "tree"

Dear Archangel Michael, here is my family:

? ? ?

? ? ?

Sister Brother Brother

Mother Father

You

Over the years, my family has been reduced to a minimum, so my tree has empty branches.

You will adapt your scheme to your own family composition.

The important thing is that the people you want to make peace with are on it. Now that you have a clear picture of your roots, take time to breathe deeply. The inhalation and exhalation will create a zone of emotional retreat to prepare you to receive Michael's cleansing energy.

Note: *I asked Michael if it was possible to include our deceased on the diagram, and he said it was fine. He will strive to release the pain of loss and separation while strengthening the light of the departed soul.*

The letter can be written after the exercise or a little later depending on the call of the consciousness. The soul functions on the principle of temporality of the divine world, which is precursor to knowledge.

It's normal to feel fluctuating when approaching a transformation because the process has begun in the invisible.

The body is torn between the desire to move forward and the desire to stay still. If there is a strong emotional wave, thinking about Michael will create a level of adjustment to prepare for the upliftment that is taking place.

The body of your letter should contain a few key elements, explanations that open the door to exposure:

- Family agreements or disagreements
- Common memories
- Traumatic events (separations, arguments, abandonment, etc.)
- Actions towards you (reproaches, devaluation…)
- The image that your family members reflect to you
- Perception of their word
- Feelings developed towards them

Sample letter

From

Born:

"My dear Archangel Michael,

I write to you today to free myself and understand my family ties. My body, my heart and my soul hold the traumas of my life within my family.

-

Write down each important memory/family situation to be transformed

-

Michael, my friend, can you help me understand my place in this family?
Thank you for infusing your divine energy to free me from family influences that do not belong to me.
May the cleansing power that emanates from you cleanse my body, heart and soul of all family wounds so that I can see these people (name them) with the eyes of God.
May your cleansing power help me to let go of these dramas so that we can all move forward in love and understanding. Thank you, thank you, thank you.
I trust you! I love you!"

This template is a base that you will personalize and adapt to your story.
When you do the exercise, each word should reflect and resonate with you, even if that moment seems painful. You are in a healing word action. Don't hesitate to tell everything that seems important to you, there are no unnecessary details.

To give you an idea, when I was 8 years old, I liked to put a different outfit on my favorite doll every day. Once I put her in an outfit consisting of a pink fringed jacket, a dress I had sewn for her and her boots. She looked so beautiful...

My little sister decided to play with my doll, I didn't like to lend her my toys because she wasn't paying attention at all... Ordinary children's bickering as it can happen in all siblings... I had no desire to give her my dolly this day and for once I remember saying no.

Crying fit... she went to complain to my father about my refusal... Our toy box was full, there were other dolls, but she had decided she needed this one... Predictably, my father became angry with me. In front of him, I repeated my refusal to lend it to my sister... He ripped it out of my hands, opened the bin and threw away my pretty doll to make me understand my so-called selfishness...

This anecdote is ridiculous when told in an adult voice, but for me it is a memory that has stayed with me. I mentioned it to Michael in my letter... All this to say don't hold back when it comes to writing, every confidence is part of you, and you will never be judged....

You are divinely assisted from start to finish and if the tears flow, don't hold them back.
The cleansing is probably already underway. Listening to your feelings is essential to receive the awareness and change of vision afterwards.
The first step of the light coaching with Michael is dedicated to a family purification work.
It's possible to include in this first letter a paragraph about karmic and transgenerational links:

"Michael, you now know the situation that concerns me regarding ... (name the family member(s) you mentioned), can you help me understand and release the ancestral influences that are disturbing my relationship with ... in this life, for the good of all. I trust you! Thank you, thank you, thank you!"

"Michael, can you help me to step back and release karmic and family influences that are preventing harmony in my life, in the life of .... (name of person involved) and in our relationship.
May light be shed on our respective paths so that we can move forward in love and respect.

I trust you! Thank you, thank you, thank you!"

The correspondences with the Archangels are used to verbalize and visualize to improve the quality of present life, for our existences take place in the here and now.

Too much digging into the past can lead to thoughts of fatality and prevent any positive action. However, without making extreme fixations, it is interesting to unblock certain old mechanisms to advance on the path of inner peace. The important thing is not to limit yourself and to use your feelings as a compass.

The sensations felt after writing the letter will be strictly personal and different from one individual to another.

The old energies will be emptied and then regenerated afterwards, personally this is the feeling I had.

In my case, I felt like Michael was vacuuming my body and all the old dust was finally coming off.

I went through a bit of a fog as the understandings came one after another, but it was ultimately very positive as my inner and outer worlds began to change. I was able to discover answers to questions that had remained unanswered and relationships with those around me began to improve.

Long-standing conflicts calmed down; my sensitivity was balanced. Instead of internalizing and taking the attacks personally, I saw them as behavior that was not particularly directed at me. I think it taught me to live by my inner truth without letting my environment affect me.

Every effect has a cause, so I send light, kindness to people and move forward being equal to myself, no matter what the context. To pass this stage is to forge a new suit of armor to fit you. It is not assembled under the prism of fear and pain, it is not designed to hide but to protect this new emerging consciousness. Discord always passes, only love remains...

Divine Masculine

"In the Masculine, don't look for the energy of the man, find the energy of the Father..."
Archangel Michael – 2021

Divine and Universal perfection is based on the constant balance of polarities. In nature, masculine and feminine energies take turns, complementing and harmonizing each other to ensure the continuity of life cycles.
Without these two opposing poles, nothing could exist. The masculine and the feminine are part of the Divine poetry that allows the manifestation of life on Earth. After exploring family lineages, Michael's light coaching takes us a little deeper into our underground galleries to explore and balance our Divine Masculine.

The body, your Earth, has a predominantly female polarity. It is the passive, solid force. As an example, it is enough to take stock of all the shocks that our body undergoes daily (food, excess, stress...) it is a good barometer as for the capacities of adaptation and resistance of our body envelope.

The male polarity represents the forces of action, of decision, the fire in its pure state. On a physical level, this would correspond to the left side of our brain, to logic, to rationality.

From a spiritual point of view, we could speak of pure power. Michael's strategic force will come into play to harmonize our subtle polarities.

The spiritual facets of the Divine Masculine: tipping the balance of power equally. Whatever our gender, our choices or our orientations, this energetic polarity, when in harmony, is the force that anchors us in a serene daily life, in accordance with our personality and our deepest aspirations. How can we achieve this union of opposites?

I've long been interested in karmic polarities and the proven theories of incarnational balance. The argument of repetitive lives spent in one gender rather than another is credible.

Indeed, if an individual's soul has lived its previous existences mainly in female bodies and is currently living in a male body, it is likely that the balance is precarious.

The soul may find it difficult to adapt, as it deviates slightly from its usual evolutionary trajectory. The protagonist, unaware of his previous conditions, may be faced with a discomfort, a gap between himself and others that he cannot explain...

The problem with this kind of spiritual exploration is that it's too much about the past, and it becomes unnecessarily entangled.

I went through these stages to understand, I was amazed at the answers I found, but I was tired of my destiny depending on someone else's interpretation. Receiving too many different messages leads to a chain of contradictions that is more worrying than helpful… I accepted to take the instructions as they came!

I finally discovered what patience really meant. Before, the very word sounded like a punishment.

If I was told "be patient", my anger would rise, and I would be faced with an injustice designed to play on my nerves!

I came to understand that being patient was more about being actively calm... You know, when the possible outcomes no longer have any influence on the quest that you hold so dear...
You know what I mean? Getting wise is good, getting back to work is better!
What was going to happen now? The great thing about the Archangels is that you don't have to wait feverishly for a call or a message that is slow in coming. The news reports are relayed better than the best news agencies.

Michael's words that took me to the second stage of light coaching are these:

"Through weighing, I restore fairness!"

Was he referring to the fateful moment of the Last Judgment? That moment when Gabriel sounds the trumpet to awaken the righteous.
Unwittingly, I fell back into my old fears by imagining the worst-case scenario. Why burden myself with apocalyptic visions when the Highest is

overseeing everything from beginning to end? We all have a right to redemption and Heaven; we can even get much better if we are open to the options that present themselves.

Having Michael, Gabriel, Raphael and Uriel in my life brings me closer to God every day. Achieving a high level of knowledge never replaces the fact that we are eternal learners. These wonderful beings have brought to my soul the beauties that I sought in vain to contemplate with my eyes. Restoring equity...

I had done everything in my power not to be noticed. I pandered to what was expected of me and my only outbursts of extravagance reflected the opposite of my personality.

I didn't think I was beautiful enough to consider myself a woman. As for men, I had ended up dismissing them before I even took the time to get to know them or give them a chance...

I had been conditioned so much that they would never be interested in me… I had trouble situating myself in time and space... To give ourselves a chance... I believe that this tiny detail is enough to tip the confidence in the right direction...To be aware of our place, we must fully accept our masculine and feminine sides.

I never knew where I stood in my life as a woman. As a teenager, I couldn't find clothes in my size and, even then, the mentality of the 90s dictated that a fat woman, even if she was pretty, would always be ugly... Thanks to the collective bullshit!
On the male side, the diktats were twisted. I was not allowed to be feminine, so logic dictated that I had to hide in XXL T-shirts to conceal what was not to be seen. I had to look like a tomboy, but at the same time I couldn't expect to be noticed by boys!
As a young adult, with my weight cut in half, I found myself completely lost when I started being approached by men...
Going from nothing to everything, suddenly arousing interest when you've been living in the skin of an invisible person... The psychological shock is severe!

No matter what happens to us with the opposite sex, I have always believed that the reason men and women are here on earth is because they are useful to each other. I was working with Michael on the roots of my body, my earth, I was my home, and the masculine was my foundation.

I took a sheet of paper, a pencil and started to write. My memory dictated the names of all the masculine people who had passed through my life. I looked at this list carefully, and I realized where Michael was leading me when he talked about balance and fairness.

To make peace, again, not just with myself. And to achieve this state, stepping back from it helps to understand this ME, this unexplored part of ourselves...

To finally bring out that healthy and constructive masculine force, the builder's energy that is essential to our achievements. It doesn't matter if you are a man or a woman. Gender is only a birth attribution and does not define anything. Let's focus on awakening our masculine strengths to create unity.

Here we are again at the heart of human relationships!
Unwittingly, we are constantly in separation from others. For example, our patterns do not allow us to let our guard down for a second, we are always in doubt and mistrust. We build up ideals and expectations that bring us down...
Society is turning us into easily replaceable products and if we don't keep up with it: Next!

Look at one of the most frequent requests made to Michael: Cut the negative ties!
This speaks volumes about the constant state of separation we are in... Far from the peace we long to find... Over time, I've learned to dislike the term 'cut'.
Liberate and transform is more in line with the light. Look at everyday life, if you cut yourself with a sharp object, you bleed... Apply the same example from an energetic point of view, cutting a link is the same effect. You don't see it, but the wound still bleeds. This is the politically correct way of denying the lessons of the soul, whether they are good or

bad! By weighing, I am restoring equity... Stop using the chainsaw to cut the base of the tree while letting its roots die underground...

The male influences that run through our lives are the materialization of the models we seek to build. Fathers, brothers, friends, partners, lovers, husbands...

They reassure, they vibrate the stability that we often lack. Equity forms a circle of peace within which the vibration of the new is constantly circulating. The list I had drawn up was revealing in many ways.

The names on the list gave an overview of my relationship with the opposite sex: they ranged from the indifferent to the unattainable. My Divine Masculine was in the same direction! I had dreams of construction, but I was unable to anchor them in matter

Coaching No. 2 - 2nd letter

Awaken to the power of masculine

"Be one with the builder's energy..."

Archangel Michael - 2021

The steps of the light coaching have a common thread that connects them to each other. Even if they seem to be unrelated, their order respects the evolutionary patterns of the being.

The purpose of the Divine Masculine exercise is to introduce the first vibrations of materialization before Raphael carries out a deep healing. The aim is to remove the layers of toxic energies that prevent full unfolding.

After making my list of male influences, I wrote my letter exactly like the template below. Next to each name, I mentioned the place these men have occupied in my life, without dwelling on specific facts.

However, as you write your letter, it tells your own story. If you feel the need to share a memory related to one of the names, please do so. Michael likes precision and this will reinforce his plan of action to target priority cleansing.

To complete step 1 on family ties, it is possible to name the men in your family again to trigger a further release. In this way, a new perspective is created by ridding yourself of the influences that have built you up.

Sample letter

From:

Born

"My dear Archangel Michael,

I write to you today to ask for help and understanding regarding my Divine Masculine in order to harmonize my sacred Earth.

The masculine influences that have passed through my life have played an important role in building me and who I am in the here and now. Here is a list of the men involved:

-

Please use your liberating and purifying force to harmonize my Sacred Masculine and transmute all the residual masculine energy that is now useless to me into pure loving light.
For my sake and that of the people mentioned. I am grateful for what they have given me, I am giving back to them what does not belong to me. I am building my foundations in peace.
I thank you from the bottom of my heart for your support in my evolutionary process. I have full confidence in the revelations and solutions that you will place on my path. I am taking back my full power! I trust in you! Thank you, thank you, thank you! I love you!"

You will have to be very attentive to the energies that will be transmitted to you following this work. Michael will send you very powerful waves which may manifest in different ways depending on the person.
For myself, a few minutes after writing the letter, I felt the need to get up and leave my office.
I felt as if a force was grabbing me by the shoulders and pulling me upwards.

At my root chakra, a current began to flow and gradually rose into my belly. It was strong, comforting and beautiful, I was torn between wanting to keep it to myself and needing to let it out.

I put on some music, a random song from my playlist and from the first notes I started to dance. My body movements adapted to this new energy, I didn't care if what I was doing was right or wrong, because I could feel the space being created inside... I had a new vision of giving/receiving.

Everything I thought I had offered in my life seemed abstract because I realized that it came from my conditioning and not from me. I obeyed the law of circulation; I received in that moment a magical and salutary energy. By deploying it through the dance I gave it back to the universe so that it would return it to me tenfold.

The masculine and the energy of the warrior took their place...

Behind the scenes, this work was just a drop in the ocean. Michael's talents in harmonizing this aspect

of my life were just the small spark that prepared me for what I was to experience with Raphael.
The toxic past was leaving me, so that I could remember only the best!

The thought forms

"What the other person thinks is theirs, you are free to refuse it..."

Archangel Michael – 2021

The third stage of Michael's light coaching ends with the thought forms. This moment is a strong symbol, it marks the renewal of the earth, the deepest rebel roots have disappeared.
The water will finally be able to emerge from its subsoil to irrigate the space abundantly.
Like Mother Nature who takes over the seasons, the energies follow a perfectly orchestrated mechanism: transforming the useless into useful, introducing the full after a period of emptiness.

The work of awareness carried out so far is bearing fruit, the deep cleaning has left the earth fallow.
For the transformation to continue, there is still one element that must not be neglected to complete the process: the dissolution of thought-forms.
Also called egregores, these are program issued by the collective to shape the perception and behavior of the majority.
These programs, most often erroneous, insinuate themselves and crystallize in the unconscious. They then become tenacious beliefs that become anchored in the mind of their host.

The best-known forms of groupthink are, for example, religions. Generations of people have nurtured these dogmas for centuries to bring light into the darkness of those who need it.
Other types of egregores are programmed to cause major upheavals, the case of wars for example. They represent the darker side of the groupthink form. These lower group instincts are motivated by jealousy, envy, greed, the need for domination… These two cases are the most common examples,

but the thought form applies to many situations. The seed is planted by a leader whose voice is a little louder than his or her peers...
This is the double-edged sword; this voice can inspire or destroy. It is very important to discern the intention behind the message...

We live in a society of egregores. Fashions, for example, are thought forms that help us define our tastes and preferences. Some of them inspire us, elevate us and make us better. On the other hand, ideas, conceptions, judgements are thought forms that dictate morality to us without considering our inner truths.

We are born as a "virgin", the soul already has its spiritual and emotional roadmap, however, the unconscious is not yet confronted with the repetition of memories. As we grow, we are subjected to thought forms from outside. Over time, these become embedded in the mind to create a distorted perception of who we really are. Thought is a powerful source of energy. Its foundation is transmission. Used wisely, it is the trigger for great enlightenment and leads to benevolent sharing. Misdirected, it becomes a weapon of mass destruction and causes division. In close, friendly, professional or social circles, thought forms are not always intended to harm.

Relationships with others are complex, it is the main subject we study in the school of life. Sometimes people think they know us better than we know ourselves.
They share hours, days, years, a life... they take the time to observe us and willingly share their opinion, their feelings about us. They see us as capable or incapable... At the bend in the road, malevolent people will enter the scene.
They will ruin our lives and leave consequences...

Like everyone else, I haven't escaped the conditioning dictated by others. I gave them so much importance...
I became withdrawn, sensitive, too emotional... After the teaching on the family and the divine

masculine, I was looking forward to Michael's next instructions.

I had taken to writing down my progress in a notebook to see how I was doing. I could already see that the stress and fear were gone. I no longer woke up in the morning with my stomach in knots, I felt like I was in a warm, protective cocoon. For me, it was a real miracle!

"Think outside the box..."

Michael's words made me think of the Sphinx submitting riddles. At first, I thought about standing out from the crowd. If I thought about it, my physical appearance had already done that for me, much to my despair...

What was he getting at? It's always like that, when you meet an obstacle, you focus on it so much that you forget what's around it.

I needed a sign because my brain was trying to decipher the hidden meaning of the sentence but in vain... I think my dear Michael was sorry to see me rowing like that because he eventually came to my rescue. If the message doesn't get through, our friends in the light will use every channel at their disposal to help us. Who said that the Archangels were conventional? I think they are very hip in their own way!

My epiphany came via the phone. It was a Monday morning; my mobile phone on the table, I suddenly saw the screen switch to music mode and select a random song...

It was a famous girl's band hit from the 90's... My God, I hadn't listened to this song since I was a teenager... The upbeat rhythm of the song took me back to a time I really wanted to forget...

During my childhood and teenage years, I had big problems with my weight. I was aware of my physical difference from others. Going to school in the 90s while being obese was no walk in the park.

The icons of the time were sexy, free and extravagant girls... It was fashionable among students to look like these glittering stars. Platform shoes, crop tops and low-rise trousers were the standard attire for being part of the "elite". In other words, with my sad appearance, I had no chance to

join the popular clan... Not only did I have to be invisible, but I was constantly told that because I was fat, no boy would ever like me...
It's amazing what 12-year-olds with changing hormones can do or say! Face it and shut up, put your head down and let the insults pass. Every school day was a never-ending nightmare...

The breaking point came one day in class. At that time, I was very attracted to Ray, one of the boys in my class. He was a bit of a star, only dating popular girls who met the beauty standards required in 1996. I had told a classmate about my attraction to this boy behind my back; she told everyone this little scoop. I became even more of a target for humiliating remarks.
One morning, during a history-geography class, I started to hear snickering around me. Pellets were being thrown at me, I guess the words written inside were not flattering. At one point the teacher, annoyed, called for silence and one of the girls in the class shouted, "Isa is in love with Ray". There was a general burst of laughter, 27 pairs of eyes full of

contempt turned towards me. The teacher laughed too and punished me by asking me to leave.

I ran across the room in tears under a shower of paper pellets... Being thrown out of class so unjustly finally anchored in me the conviction that I could never be loved by anyone...

With a hammer and chisel, the thought forms took hold of me and implanted themselves firmly in my skull. Thinness could only be a VIP invitation to a paradise to which I had no access. Being thin was synonymous with happiness, love, beauty, success...

I was ridiculous to believe this back because no human being is spared from pain, even the most physically perfect... So much guilt had a negative impact on my balance. One consequence led to another, and I ended up rejecting myself completely. It was impossible for me to see any beauty in myself.

To the outside world, I was a monster, a pile of fat, I had to suffer in silence... I had not yet experienced the discovery of my body and my femininity, and I was conditioned to believe that I was too much because I had committed the horrible crime of being different...

Especially since at that time I would have given anything to be normal... I had to hide, and I was not allowed to be in love because I was not beautiful.

I was forbidden to do so, and if a boy had been interested in me, he would have become a laughingstock. I would have dragged him down with me!

"Think outside the box" I could finally see what Michael was getting at! It wasn't about being forward thinking, but about never forgetting that other people's opinions don't define me.

The thought forms were so big that they came alive in my mind and my internal perception.

All this repetitive talk triggered a brainwashing that disconnected me from my light source. No one wakes up one morning and suddenly decides they are ugly, stupid, insignificant, etc.

How can you see yourself in a good light when you hear all the time "you won't make it", "this is not the right decision", "you should do it this way" ....

These egregores that invade us do not belong to us in the end, they are the mirror of various insecurities! Holding up the banner of a pseudo-truth allows the other person to reassure themselves by saying, "I found someone weaker than me!"
Attack is sometimes the best defense....
To paraphrase, the other person plants an already rotten seed in your soil and your sensitivity naively lets it flourish. In time, that seed will grow into an angry, extinct flower if you are not careful. In the end, it is not the outside world that prevents us from shining.

We are simply channeling energies in the wrong way by giving them a place that is not theirs. We entertain thoughts that are not our own.
I used to look at myself in the mirror automatically, making a list of the physical and moral flaws that had been pointed out to me. Aware of everything that is wrong with me.
Hearing this song after decades woke me up. I felt I had no choice but to accept what was being done to me, when it had always been done to me... My best

protection was time and oblivion… I ran into the bathroom and stood in front of the mirror. At first, I could hardly stand my own gaze. I felt as if I were seeing those eyes for the first time...

Gradually, I saw a light that just wanted to shine. I felt my heartbeat in my chest, I gently put my hand there, I wanted to bury the hatchet...

I didn't exist. At least the label the others had tried to put on me. It wasn't real!

I had a right; I am a part of God's creation just like the others. I had allowed all this to exist and if they had shown a cruel lack of indulgence towards me, I did not have to inflict it on myself in return.

Freeing myself from family burdens, balancing the masculine and now detaching myself from thought forms.... So far, the path was perfect to clearly mark the break between me and the fixed patterns!

Coaching No. 3 - 3rd letter

Turn off the thought forms and turn them back to light.

"I will lead my armies into your battlefield, together we will reverse oppression..."
Archangel Michael – 2021

The light coaching now leads you to the reclaiming of your personality, free of any guilt or devaluation.
The first step in your evolutionary staircase is almost complete. Michael will put his energy at your disposal to open the door to a benevolent sanctuary that is still unknown to you: trust.
This last turn may be difficult to negotiate as emotional outbursts are possible. Exploring the shadows caused by thought forms is like exposing yourself.
In your letter, don't be afraid to be a victim, the impact of thoughtforms on personal development

affects everyone on different scales. We are always victims, of others but above all of ourselves, which is the most difficult thing to recognize.
Tell the events and feelings as you experienced them, without taboo or restraint. This method is very effective in bringing ego wounds to light and gaining perspective on them. If you feel the need to write your letter in several parts, don't hesitate. Don't worry about being perfect, just be yourself.

Nothing is harmless, know that thought forms include all the repetitive prohibitions that have built barriers, beliefs that force you to deny yourself.

Some examples to inspire you, it's up to you to let your experience speak for itself afterwards:

- You have different tastes from others, so you were called to order to put you back on the right track
- Your appearance, your preferences, your choices did not fit the mold
- You were conditioned and directed in ways that did not suit you

- Your creativity, your personality has been restricted. You have long held secret desires in your heart
- You have made changes at the insistence of others
- You feel totally out of step with what you have become and what you really like
- Everyone gives their opinion when you present a project, they tell you it won't work
- You are constantly compared to others; the focus is always on what you lack and not what you have
- You are put in boxes: you are timid, shy, egotistical... so you can't go against your nature
- You are encouraged to change but at the same time you are discouraged by being told that you have a lot of work to do on yourself etc.

Sample letter:

From:

Born:

"My dear Archangel Michael,

I thank you for your presence and your unfailing support in the path of transformation of my earth. I write to you today to ask for your help once again.

I finally realize the light that exists within me, so that it can shine fully I submit to you the blocking and paralyzing thought forms that have kept me in a false vision of myself....

-

-

Michael, I trust your intelligence and your liberating power! Can you infuse me with a new level of understanding and detachment from those patterns that have prevented full self-expression?

Thank you for liberating me, for purifying me of what needs to be purified so that I may enter my mission of incarnation, that in alignment with my soul. I am taking possession of my own personality again, with complete

confidence. For my good and that of all. Thank you, thank you, thank you!
I trust in you, in us! I love you!"

I cried a lot during the exercise, the tears were flowing but I felt a sense of calm in my heart. In truth, my anger was false. In fact, I was not angry at anyone but myself for adding so much oxygen to the pyre of my detractors…
Today, I don't care what people think of me. Life is like that; you can't love everyone no matter what you say and fortunately!
It doesn't matter if they think I'm incapable or on a predestined path…After all, what forces me to cooperate? Nothing!
Don't ever let anyone divert you from your path of light. Those who control others are only frightened children. Let us not entertain their behavior, let us only pray for their upliftment!

Moment of gratitude

"Your progress is change, your progress is mine, if you look back you will feel my presence..."
Archangel Michael – 2021

The first part of the light coaching with Michael ends here for the moment. The earthly issues that have been worked on are some of the most difficult to overcome. From now on, the voice of the ego, the restlessness, will take up less space.

Before beginning the intuitive ascension with Gabriel, it is legitimate to wonder if the purifications and transmutations acquired will last. It's normal to be afraid of falling back into the old patterns that directed us before. In my personal experience, I sometimes have flashes of the "old me" but they are ephemeral and above all no longer correspond to my current mentality.
While Michael is now passing the baton to the incredible Messenger, his work with you does not stop.

The connection between you and him is firmly established. He will be the "bridge" that will assist others in the next stages of coaching to help you reach your spiritual goal.

Don't be discouraged, if a "problem" arises it is because your soul is able to solve it. Michael has fulfilled his mission by teaching you detachment. Never doubt this truth: you will always be guided. A possible backtracking does not mean a failure.

Only our ego has a strong opinion on the matter... Honestly, I don't think anyone fails, we just take healthy breaks.

The archangels form a team of which you are now a part. For example, if you are in a healing phase with Raphael and your thoughts are not in tune, Gabriel will put signs in your path and Uriel will clarify your thoughts. You are not alone!

However, it is a proof of immense love towards our luminous friends to want to keep intact the achievements accumulated after a work. It is a great sign of respect for them and for you (the barriers have fallen; you are beginning to see yourself in a new light).

It's possible to write a bonus letter to Michael to thank him for his great contribution to your well-being and thus anchor the results obtained:

"My dear Archangel Michael,
By your power you have assisted me. You have lent me your sword of light throughout the observation, understanding and liberation of my promised land. In this crucial stage of my personal development, you have opened my vision and my consciousness, closing my old life cycles. I feel rejuvenated and liberated. Your divine intervention has brought me closer to my source, reconnecting me to my origins in light. Your power protects the teachings and results I have achieved and continues to act in the here and now. Like you, Godlike, I move forward under your guidance in love, harmony and justice, for my good, for the good of all. I trust you and so be it! Thank you, thank you, thank you! I love you!"

This letter is the verbalization of your liberation.

You are affirming and anchoring in matter the benefits you have received. It symbolizes the fact that you have not invited Michael into your life for a fixed period.

You haven't simply asked him for a favor, you are returning his help fairly by allowing him to assist you in times of need. You maintain an active and fluid connection.

With a prayer, you make an occasional request.

With this letter you involve and acknowledge the support of the Archangels in your life. They are your special friends in whom you have faith, in whom you believe!

From now on, what happens next depends only on your goodwill, for the powers of heaven are devoted to your cause!

CHAPTER 15

Born and reborn

Gabriel - God is my strength

« In the silence of the night I listen…
In the distance, a sound, unintelligible to the ear, from the Highest, The darkness wanted to take me away, you were there, On the road of illusions, you showed me understanding,
Mixture of fear and ecstasy, I could not go against the will. On the way to myself, I met you... Gabriel… »

Water - Fluidize, fertilize, bloom

"Do you feel this echo vibrating far away? Keep your heart intact, clear your mind and let the Father's whispers rise to him. Then you will discover the truth that is yours"

Archangel Gabriel – 2021

From the earth springs water, these two elements coexist in perfect complementarity.

First underground, it rises from the depths to fulfil its irrigation functions in nature. More than 70% of our planet is made up of water. It is divided into oceans, seas, lakes and rivers. Where the earth is raw and arid, water is the power of life in its purest form. The source of everything, it illustrates the cycles of conception, gestation and birth.

As humans, we respect this order. The union of bodies and the mixing of male/female fluids create matter. Our development takes place in a liquid environment before we are expelled into the daylight. Thus, making our grand entrance into the theatre of life. Water will then contribute to the balance of our vital functions. In its liquid state, in its calmest form, water is fluid and fertile.

Unleashed, it becomes the force that destroys to purify. Transformed into ice, it freezes the course of things to prepare the next cycle.

Versatile, this element inexorably continues its work, free of all constraints. A symbol with a double meaning, its goodness is matched only by its anger.

The phenomenon of storms is one of the examples that show us the unpredictable character of water and the amplitude of its action.

Gabriel is the most mysterious Archangel in the celestial kingdom. The writings are unanimous on his role as a messenger of God. He is the bearer of news that has changed the course of history forever. A prince of light and cold, his intellectual power makes him a discreet Archangel. Gabriel works in the shadows, the signs of his presence at our side are very subtle. He exposes himself to the eyes when he is mandated for divine missions of the highest importance. He does not need to seek the full light, for every part of him is composed of it.

He is the holder of the highest divine secrets. Michael "God-like" is the energy of focused and precise action, Gabriel is the intellectual force.

Moreover, the two Archangels were present at the destruction of the city of Sodom, it took no less than the iron hand and the velvet glove to accomplish this task. He is the spirit that lends its hand to the sword, the water that waters the earth!

A true free electron, his power extends to infinity and is not limited to a simple role of messenger. Like the water that flows unceasingly, its fluid represents the purest creative process. The seed of life that emerges from the earth to blossom into light. As humans, we tend to put up barriers between Gabriel and ourselves.

His splendor, his presence, sometimes makes him misunderstood by ordinary people. Gabriel is like a star that we admire from afar but cannot approach.

Despite a certain reluctance towards him, Gabriel's Force is inside each of us and is none other than intuition, which is the totality of the soul's knowledge.

I mentioned the act of procreation, which is the action leading to fertilization, and intuition is the mysterious aspect of it, the sleeping water, the inexplicable knowledge on which we cannot put words. Its role is to be the invisible thread that links us to God's plans from life to life. Following it allows our greatest aspirations to be born and to materialize. Repressing it or diverting it to serve

obscure purposes makes it the architect of our "misfortunes", if we can call them that...
Water, Gabriel and intuition form the core of our trinity, that magic we find hard to believe in!
Our earthly vision is unconditionally resigned to the visible and palpable vicissitudes of existence. Hence the automatism of turning first to Michael. Since he deals with the concrete side of a problem, he seems more accessible.

Everything that touches the invisible fascinates and frightens. This out-of-control guidance follows its own laws, its own timing, confronting us with divine truths that we refuse to hear. Judgement can then be unquestionable, as the ego encourages us to double-lock the doors without allowing us to open them. From this point of view, it is easy to understand our reserve towards the Messenger who is nevertheless a precious ally...

After Michael's teaching, which was intense and productive, I took a short break. I needed a time of regeneration to sort out the transformations that had already taken place. They were subtle. Now I couldn't boast about winning the lottery, radically changing my life or finding the right man, but I didn't care. I was learning to live again; I was smiling, and I was much more dynamic.

I was no longer suffering but taking life in my stride. The material rewards were coming, I knew.
I prepared for the activation of favorable circumstances by reshuffling my chessboard. I felt like I was flying, and I liked it. I was sure that Gabriel's trumpet would sound, not to judge me but to give me the start of the next coaching session.
Of the four, he is my undisputed favorite! His presence is imposing, his aura is royal and his energy strips us of all lies...

In Provence, the last days of November marked the beginning of the Christmas festivities. I'm always happy at this time of year because I can gorge myself on white chocolate, make tons of gift packages and live in a fairytale setting. As a kid I used to look forward to December, when the toy catalogues arrived in the letterbox there was general euphoria because it meant we could phone Santa and order the presents we wanted under the tree.

My parents didn't like this kind of phone call so much, especially when they got the phone bill in January... The most vivid memory for me will always be the Provençal cot that my mother made. The big buffet in the dining room would look festive as it hosted this little show for a limited time.

The statue of Michael was temporarily moved for the occasion. I remember that he was put on the pedestal table where the telephone was placed. I liked to wrap a piece of garland around his neck, it made him look like a cabaret actor... He would tell me during our work together that he had smiled at this childish whim.

When my mother took out the boxes containing the Santons for the cot, I would sit next to her to look at these treasures that were only born once a year. I liked the animals and the wise men very much, I took them in my little hands to observe them from every angle, being careful not to drop them.

Emptied of its usual ornaments, the buffet was gradually transformed into a replica of Bethlehem. My mother put all her heart into it, she spent hours composing each hill, each alley, placing correctly the starry sky paper she bought for the occasion...
When the decor was finished, the houses and the characters took their annual place to enchant the young and old!

The second to last santon to join the assembly was a blond angel with outstretched wings, his hands clasped in a gesture of prayer. This one had a special place, my mother placed it on top of a paper mountain created especially for it. This "angel moment" as I called it, was the highlight of the show for me. Seeing my admiration, my mother used to say to me:
"It's the Archangel Gabriel, he came to announce to Mary that she would be the mother of Jesus! He's up there protecting the people in the cot and he can watch over the successful birth of Jesus."
My little girl's heart always had a soft spot for the Christmas angel who lit up her village... Gabriel...

I think my attachment to Gabriel comes from the fact that he reminds me of the beautiful white angel of my childhood. Contrary to the spiritual fashions that push us to know more and more, I never sought to know his identity.
I know now that he has always been there, despite the years when I turned my back on him. He is one of those reassuring friends who can be counted on in times of need.

The prospect of working with Gabriel made me happy, it was like reliving my early years of spiritual carefreeness... Yet his frankness is disconcerting, but he never hurts anyone! He is a luminous being of rare finesse and elegance, with such a degree of evolution... He makes the beauties of the soul accessible and easy to understand. God couldn't have chosen a more beautiful messenger!
Opinions differ as to his physical appearance. Some mediums and mystics describe him as a woman and religious writings present him as a man. It would be presumptuous to try to decide on this matter by seeking to favor one view over another. Spiritual

experience is an intimate matter, and Gabriel, the intermediary between God and man, can count on an androgynous side to blur the lines during his appearances.

His abilities are in his image. He has in him the masculine force in its noblest form and the Grace of the sacred feminine in its full sensitivity. Let us analyze all his missions.

As the "Saint Patron" of Communications, he oversees all artistic professions. It is the message, the accomplished action, the finished product. Because of his closeness to our Blessed Mother, he is the guardian of women and mothers. We ask for his help to bring something into being (a child, an agreement, a relationship, a project...).

He's the still hidden part of creation, the seed to be watered and nourished with faith. Between the point of departure (fertilization) and the point of arrival (completed action), Gabriel puts all his strength into it!

I was in the middle of a relaxation process when he arrived. Every evening, after the shower, I allow myself 15 minutes to lie down and breathe. Focusing on the rhythm of my breath allows me to release the toxins and tensions accumulated during the day. These moments are my "minutes of peace". During one of them, I felt two huge arms lift me up and take me to a timeless place. I was gently deposited in a kind of river of light. I was totally immersed, I could hear the splash of the water except I was not wet, and I was not cold.

The glistening current flowed along my body; its movement was not disturbed by my presence.

I heard a tinkle of bells and this message:

"Intelligence does not come from what you learn but from what you do with it!"

It was the continuation of the journey!

This vision set the tone for the new turn I was about to take. Michael's root work transformed a vacant lot into fresh soil, ready to receive his seed. Gabriel takes over to become the seed, the fertilizer and the watering can. Socially, an intelligent person will be one who is well educated and has a high level of scholarship. Proportionally, a person who learns on his own will not always be judged at his true worth. It is time to remember Michael: *"Think outside the box..."*

Intelligence is not just a matter of social background and cannot be quantified by the amount of education received!

Let's take the example of Mohammed, being illiterate did not prevent him from following Gabriel's teaching... Divine knowledge is a subtle mixture of truth, intuition and faith. There is a term for this: emotional intelligence. Alas, we are not taught this in school...

Gabriel is the loving link between the heart, belief and the expression of all innate potential. His function as a messenger will serve us here to know and integrate our soul program.

To accept truths of which we are unaware in order to tame the limiting ego. In short, to go through the storms to become a calm, flowing and fertile river!

"Don't be afraid, Mary, for you have found favor with God..."

These are the first words that Gabriel addressed to our Blessed Mother. Everyone has grace, our blinkers only prevent us from seeing it. The truth from above confronts the logic from below... Mary accepted her truth in abandonment and trust!
Who has never been assailed by guilt or doubt? How many times have you said to yourself, "I should do this, I want to do that" only to follow a path dictated by reason and filled with disillusionment and disappointment? It's more comfortable to withdraw and tell yourself that there will be other opportunities. This may be true, except in the case where regret persists... You brood, you blame yourself, you question yourself...

This is the subtlety of the Divine Messenger. With him, there is no sentence but only a reminder of what must be and will be, including that unknown which remains hidden. It may seem surreal to think that our mortal bodies are the receptacle of so many blessings. Yet, if we step back, our capacities far exceed our limits.

Let us meet the shining star at the end of the road!

Divine Feminine

"Understand the strength of your sensitivity, it is your soul's temple"

Archangel Gabriel – 2021

Transform your night into a new day... The Divine Feminine is the polarity of emotions and feelings. Grace, compassion, beauty, love are part of the programming of this soul part. Daily, the Divine Feminine is our ability to hear our inner voice clearly so that our actions are in alignment with it.

The cradle of the Divine Feminine could be found in the right brain, the creative center. To illustrate my point on this subject, I can only refer to Michelangelo who had the vision of the angel in the block of marble and sculpted it.

Decidedly! Not only are angels everywhere, but they always put us on the path with synchronicities that are easy to understand!

The marble block was only the structure, the base, the masculine. What Michelangelo saw was the representation of the feminine, from which emanated beauty and truth... Which is really... The will that supports the vision.

Michael's help in harmonizing the Divine Masculine had reconnected me to power. I no longer felt dependent on others to build me up. I used to be the kind of person who didn't finish what I started; on a personal level, I mean... I was all fired up at the beginning and always found an excuse later to give up. Now I'm organized and I don't rush into the first trap that comes along.

"Intelligence does not come from what you learn but from what you do with it!"

These words dazzled me while awakening an old guilt. I remembered all the times I had been unable to find the right balance. Those moments of shame

at not knowing how to defend myself, at not knowing what to do... I never wanted to take revenge on the wickedness of others, I always found this type of manipulation sordid and ridiculous!
Being tolerant and accepting of everything made me a doormat to be trampled on without remorse.
I assimilated my life lessons by staying at the same level as those who "taught" me... In trying to develop myself, I didn't seek help in the right place.
Thus, my knowledge was of no use to me because I remained stuck on what I was experiencing… Gabriel knew the answers...

He knows better than anyone how to separate the true from the false... Being faced with truths that implied my responsibility was not easy to hear... I took out my notepad, got a cup of coffee and started to write: Why can't I be me? Instantly, he said to me:
"You can't want what you reject!
What you think is yours is not yours! What you don't see is yours! Be what you are!
He wanted it that way! Then you will be blessed, and His arms will be open wide!"

He understood me so well...
I couldn't stand who I was, so I rejected myself. Unattainable goals that were not for me made me feel better. I was a master at maintaining the vicious circle. I knew I was heading for the wall, but it was more comfortable for me to not admit it. Intelligence comes from the source, and to make the best use of this ability, one must learn to look at both sides of the card. The balance of the Divine Feminine activates the energies we need to take our place. Knowing how to positively resonate with our truth without letting anyone impose anything.
What did I bring to others and what did they bring to me? What were my emotions, my feelings in those moments? What qualities did I notice in my relationships? Did they correspond to what I want to see in myself? Where is the breaking point, the limit?
One by one, the neon lights lit up in my head.
On my highway, all the branches under construction started to connect. This illumination made me forget Gabriel's presence. He was still there, patient, watching me think.

I thanked him and his last word was this:
"It's in the confidence of the Father that you must do your work…"

Coaching No. 4 - 4th letter

Awakening to sensitivity of Divine Feminine

"Feminine is your will and his, put together..."
Archangel Gabriel - 2021

The Divine Masculine characterizes the "power", connecting to the Divine Feminine activates the "will" that are rooted in our interactions with ourselves and others. When the Divine Feminine is lacking, our interpretation of life suffers.
It is a reflecting mirror of our deepest torments, our embellished flaws, our duality.
The fourth exercise of light coaching will be devoted to the recurring qualities and defects that you have

encountered in your life. It's common in our relationships to put the other person's qualities on a pedestal. Unconsciously, they refer us to that personal ideal that we have set for ourselves and that seems impossible to achieve.

At the slightest sign of failure, opposition arises. If things end badly, we are then blinded by what went wrong instead of reaching a thoughtful and dignified consensus. We spend our time looking for what we lack in others. I think it's more reasonable to conclude that we have it all at the base, it's the ego that feeds the idea of lack.

We are often accused of energy vampirism, except that the search for the ideal is a by-product of this... without the bad intentions of course! As a result, imbalances appear and develop.

Let me give you a simple example:

If a product is fashionable, everyone wants it. Of course, the manufacturer has developed a simple and effective marketing strategy to limit the available stock. At first, you don't feel concerned by the general craze, but gradually you realize that this object would be perfect for you. Alas, the death knell of the stock shortage has sounded...

So begins a never-ending crusade, fueled by the hope of finding that rare pearl that everyone is praising. Then the big day arrives, the unexpected, the unhoped-for: you manage to find the coveted dream object.

You open your parcel impatiently and suddenly the euphoria disappears... disappointment! The product looks great in the photos or advertisements, but you realize that it's not so great. In our case, one could almost say that this object you fought so hard for is actually very common...

Unwittingly, you have vamped yourself with an ideal that does not exist. The field of emotions and relationships is no exception to this rule. By neglecting many details, we end up seeking a universal perfection that distracts us from the one we have within us.

In the example of the exhausted grail, the emotions (the desire to possess the object) that were generated caused you to completely miss the fact that the product may not be for you or fit your lifestyle.

Remember the strength of thought forms... Channeling and balancing the feminine polarity will focus on the "will".
The "power" worked with Michael changed the view of what seemed to be ingrained and inescapable. Here the "will" is the source, the feminine, the initial project. Gabriel's strength will intervene to bridge the gap between "will" and "capacity".
Intelligence will be the axis that keeps the two sides of the scale in balance. As with the exercise on the family and the Divine Masculine, some preparatory notes are needed to highlight the points that will be made in your letter.

You are going to repeat the list of men you submitted to Michael previously. This time you will add the names of the women in your life. You will briefly describe the feelings, emotions, qualities, flaws that the personalities of these men and women inspired in you. All our relationships have something in common, so it is likely that there will be a few traits that will feature prominently on your list. This is the big picture of what you think you are and what you reject. If you want to investigate further, you can create two lists like this one:

- **The ideal, the origins, the causes**

This is the set of reasons that attracted you to a person, relationship, situation. The positive sides, what you have without necessarily knowing how to express it. **Example:** The ability to listen, benevolence, audacity, kindness, calm, gentleness, stability, generosity...

- **Powers, effects, dominance**

Unpleasant realizations that have distanced you from a person, relationship, situation. The negative reflections of the mirror, the devaluation amplified through the other, the sources of blockage. **Example:** The dominating side, anger, instability, selfishness, coldness...

Now that these paradoxes are highlighted, Gabriel has carte blanche to deactivate the regressive spirals of repetitive emotional situations. This is an exercise that may seem long and tedious. Take as much time as you need to do it in accordance with your inner guidance.

Sample letter:

From:

Born:

"My dear Archangel Gabriel,

You, powerful messenger of God, I write to you today to ask for your strength in my process of reconnection to the Divine Feminine. Help me to bring forth the Divine Intelligence that lives within me so that inner truth is my only path. I submit to you the names of the men and women who have passed through my life.

These relationships have generated the following emotions:

-

The consequences in my relationships were as follows:

-

Michael's energy restored my "powers". For the connection to be complete, can you bring out the awareness of my "wills"?
Can you balance my wills, my feelings to manifest them healthily in my relational reality, with myself and with others?
I now have the sacred knowledge that aligns my Divine Feminine. Emotions, lacks, causes and consequences that do not belong to me are transformed into the highest vibration. I am strength, I am intuition, for my good and the good of all.
I trust in you, in me, in us.
Thank You, Thank You, Thank You! I love you!"

Gabriel's energy will spread in the form of currents of harmony that will flow through your body. You will be able to hear sounds, feel heat waves, be surrounded by pure white light...
Each reaction is different and personal. Abandon analysis, live in the moment, your body is the compass! Instructions to get the parts of your life that need it back on track will gradually come.
New ideas and desires surface...

For my part, I felt a bit lost. I can't say how long it took for the alignment to happen. During the light coaching, every day is different and passes by at a crazy speed.
The red flags went down one after the other and I started to develop healthy attitudes towards myself. I identified what I really wanted and what I no longer wanted. At that time, I was in a professional situation that made me anxious. I didn't dare to act. My intuition told me to stop the massacre and logic encouraged me to continue.
I was a freelancer, and the health crisis we went through did not help my business to grow. My option was to invest personal money to try and keep the already leaky ship afloat... It was clearly suicide!

I woke up one morning and made a firm and final decision to stop my activity. I didn't want to continue to get stuck in a situation that didn't suit me. I had invested a lot of time and energy…
I delayed deciding because I was afraid that I would still be seen as a loser. It was just a reflection of my

ego! What was better? To put myself in danger or to be free? the opinion of others or my own?
I opted for freedom and didn't give a damn about what people would say. By working on my relational patterns, I accomplished the symbolic act that closed years of erroneous wills. In a fortnight, all my applications to stop working were validated. A real record when you know that France is known for its administrative slowness... I felt such relief.

Acting in line with my feelings created the ideal circumstances in the matter. I didn't know where I was going next, but in any case, I had accomplished something that made me proud.
Quite the kind of conscious reaction I would never have had before. Gabriel's help allowed me to compare the relationship patterns I had experienced and to understand that my professional choices were in the same direction.
Through this action, my true "will" was transformed into a healthy and aligned "power". The circle was closed!

Find your style...

"Inspiration is found in the unknown, what you discover there is up to you."
Archangel Gabriel –2021

Life doesn't make us all equal, but heaven has distributed light equally. Lifestyles drag us into a long half-sleep where our creativity gradually retreats. Caught up in a moving train, we forget our true needs to adapt in a world hungry for change. Society encourages us to become chameleons.

Our senses are constantly under siege to match our interests with those of the majority.

Diversity is omnipresent, but it remains "locked" into groups that require certain criteria for integration. Barriers are built up and one might think that people are afraid to mix.

Finding your style in these conditions is a difficult task. Fortunately, nothing is impossible for the valiant lightworker!

Embarking on the path to wellness requires confidence in oneself and in one's ability to succeed, except that the specter of comparison hangs over our heads...

Before internet, our identification criteria were limited to television, magazines or our entourage.

Today, social networks are the showcases that impose the codes. A massive intrusion that gives life to trends as quickly as it buries them!

You must live with the times... I'm not criticizing the technological boom; I just feel out of step with it. Me, the 2.0 hermit!

A week after working on the Divine Feminine, I felt my energies running at full speed. My voice became clearer, I was able to synchronize my thoughts and words. My inner listening was stronger, I wanted to change my mind and make plans.

One night I woke up at 1:11am with the goal of going shopping. I took my laptop and checked my email, there was nothing interesting until I noticed a newsletter from a Parisian label announcing their "Archives".

I really like the style of their designs, but I had never ordered before, being a very loyal customer of a

competing brand. I clicked on the link to the website and started scrolling through the items on my screen. Suddenly, my attention is drawn to a blouse. For a long time, I walked with a hunched back and, from a sartorial point of view, I only wore black...
In this case, the blouse in question was printed on a sky-blue background. What were the patterns on this blouse? Lilies!
I couldn't help but laugh, I quickly realized who directed me to this item. Among his many talents, Gabriel is an image consultant in his spare time.
Suddenly I hear:

"Wear his splendor with pride"

I didn't tell anyone about my work with the Archangels. I wanted to enjoy the wonders of light coaching without having to discuss it with the outside world. For the first time in my life, it was my own moment and I wanted to keep my secret. Talk is silver but silence is golden!
The miracle of inner transformation can only work in discretion. I'm not the kind of girl who looks for

signs, I have learned to let them come to me. Waking up at a mirror hour, checking the website of a brand whose name has something to do with angels, spotting a blouse printed with lily flowers whose model name is Aura... The indications from above are sometimes surprising!

I was getting the best advice. It was working, I knew it in my gut!

Gabriel's nightly message could only be one piece of the puzzle. You will see for yourself, we spend our lives looking for the right methods to improve ourselves and when we discover the one that works, we feel less lost. The subtlety of the thread that connects each step is magical.

Style is not just about what you show people, it is a revelation of what you are trying to hide. The creativity of the Divine Feminine that we twist to please the many.

Learning to sharpen one's sense of observation and feeling supported by the best ambassadors of the sky develops a totally new vision. Wearing His splendor with pride does not only mean changing from the inside. Starting to feel in tune is a giant step, but if it is not reflected on the outside, it is like having one foot on the edge of a precipice.

Our looks are incidental to the image we project. However, there are no half measures, the appearance demon "Mythogram" encourages us to bet everything on the visual to fit the mold.

The unification of the Masculine/Feminine forms a bridge between the different inner parts that make up us, and the logical consequence is to let that unique charisma that belongs only to you shine.

I thought about all the things I loved in life in relation to what I had become. When I was younger, I loved everything to do with art. Colors, shapes, volumes... All that raw beauty that emanates from things, objects or beings. I dreamed of cooking, writing, painting... Art is a sharing of love that does not care about rules, it touches those who need it and know how to look beyond appearances.

My adult life has been the antithesis of my initial tastes. To wear its splendor proudly, I had to BE! Find my style!

Coaching No. 5 - 5th letter

Your style is yours alone!

"Don't describe yourself, express who you are...
Words are futile when vibration can say more..."
Archangel Gabriel - 2021

Finding one's style is a pivotal step in light coaching. You firmly anchor the alignment of the Masculine/ Feminine and the new vibrations received.

Gabriel has an important place in the process. The energy he will use for you will bring you out of the internalization and into the manifestation.

The radiation of your aura changes, you begin to occupy space and your charisma increases. I saw this moment as a gestation. The ovum has been fertilized, the fetus is developing and growing, it is preparing to integrate this world.

Let's agree, finding your style will not make you look like others. That's not the point!

It's about assuming your tastes to add your personal touch to who you are and what you do.

You learn to ignore the majority in order to live an existence that you like. If you think you can't do it, if you think you're boring, banal, different, marginal, not cool enough, misunderstood, outdated, out of the system... If you think that style is for the young, that you are too old... Well, you're wrong!
You are a masterpiece since the day you were born, and you will remain so until you die!

I will give you an example to help you understand how the exercise works:
Let's take the case of art in general, it's the field in which opinions diverge the most (if we exclude politics). A film, a book, a song, an exhibition... You either love it or you hate it, it's a matter of perception.
There's something for everyone! Some creations will reach a large audience and others will have less visibility, but does this prevent the artist from "being"? Absolutely not!
Why? Because he integrates his universe into his creation!
Gabriel's message is clear: "Wear His Splendor with pride". Which means: How can you create and wear

a project, a child, a relationship, an exciting job, a wedding, your dream home, travel, abundance....
If you don't create YOU? This line of thinking will help you to stop procrastinating, you are considering putting yourself first.
To prepare for writing your letter, you will answer the following questions:

- How do I see myself now?
- What is my current personality?
- Where has it all led me?
- What are my tastes and preferences?
- What did I like as a child?
- How was I influenced?
- What were the consequences in my life?
- What did I refuse, reject, forget, banish to conform to others?

Now Gabriel can act to make your style blossom!

Sample letter

From:

Born:

"My dear Archangel Gabriel,

First, I wanted to thank you for the clarifications that led me to the letter I am writing you today.

My body and my inner listening are merging, it is the turn of my deep personality to emerge. After a moment of introspection, it is in all sincerity that I note

-

- Write the answers to the above questions in the body of the letter

Gabriel, thank you for being present in my life. Thank you for infusing your divine strength to consolidate the unification of my body, heart and soul according to the perfect plan. Thank you for blossoming my style and my ability to design what is good for me and in tune with me so that my light is and shines.

I try, I go, I do! I trust your advice, your action!

I receive, I accept, and I use what is transmitted to me!

Thank you, thank you, thank you! I love you!"

The effects of this exercise are multiple. Your consciousness will begin to reprogram itself to the frequency of "everything is possible" and your level of commitment will gradually rise.

You become a creator free of all constraints. It is likely that you will begin to want to change things in your reality, give yourself time to adapt and make conscious decisions.

For me, I realized that becoming an adult did not mean giving up what I loved. I was ashamed of my childish tastes for so long, adapting became a priority! A futile and absurd reaction!

First, I made a huge sorting out of my clothes, the style of most of them didn't suit me. I hallucinated the amount of money spent on trying to become someone I didn't want to be. Then I cleaned my flat of all the things that were collecting dust.

I only wanted to surround myself with beautiful memories, I kept what didn't cause weariness.

I asked Michael and Gabriel to load up these old possessions with love for their future second life and I donated everything to charity.

I added color, shimmering prints, brightness, to my wardrobe and my home... The old passions have resurfaced, I have superimposed my childish eyes with my adult vision to create MY world, the one I feel good in. Now, I assume from A to Z to be out of step with my fellow human beings.
As a French proverb says, *"Il n'y a que celui qui ne fait rien qui ne se trompe jamais"*, so I bless those who criticize, I have fun on my side.

After all, the forbidden meanings are only temporary, these false enemies are placed to serve our great causes. Everything has a meaning, and I was reading the manual that would teach me to appreciate the blessings that awaited me...
Your quirks, your sense of humor, those little flaws that you fixate on, all the things that sometimes make you feel ashamed, let them shine through to become the light of your life!

The Divine idea

"What you call the idea is the whisper of God to give meaning in your life..."
Archangel Gabriel – 2021

The idea is the seed of all art! Free and life-giving, the idea can go through several states before it is really anchored in matter.

Emotionally, it is comparable to man:

- Stable as the earth when it is fixed (belief)
- Fluid as water when followed with regularity (commitment)
- Volatile like air because of its energetic charge and the interest it can federate (action)
- Incandescent as fire when powered by passion and conviction (concretization)

The human being is the fruit of the idea. The fields of science and research have done a colossal job in tracing and explaining our origins. Less rational, myths and legends place man at the heart of magnificent tales in which he is the result of the superior imagination. The gods, in the depths of their boredom, felt the need to fashion a work reflecting their many faces. We are the one and only creation that allows them to look at their blunders with great indulgence.

Let us not forget that if the heavens teach us much, we as incarnate beings return the favor. For the principle of communicating vessels to work perfectly, water must flow in both directions.

The codes of the world of light are based on knowledge, forgiveness and love. The beings who inhabit it do not see our mistakes as a reason to blame us, it is for them an additional reason to love us... unconditionally!

The idea is a derivative branch of love, the soul's nest of skills, the perfect essence that begets the imperfect. The ultimate gift from the heavens, the one that is sometimes perceived as unfair in the eyes of men... Gabriel, the Messenger of God, always in collusion with the Creator, is responsible for relaying the decisions of the Almighty to those who are ready. His announcements prepare for grace and manifestation.

An act of love sometimes misunderstood by our mortal consciences, the spark of the idea brings you into the realm of deep faith that heals and transforms.

If we relate this to Gabriel's two previous teachings *"Intelligence does not spring from what you learn but from what you do with it"* and *"Wear His Splendor with pride"*, we can conclude that we are more than capable of doing with the starting package we have been given. How do we use it to its full potential?

With this short tirade I got my answer: *"You know how to do what you don't know how to do yet!"*

Gabriel may not be as lyrical as Uriel, but he is not without style!

My knowledge of karma and the origins of the soul helped me a lot to understand the meaning of this message. Indeed, when one speaks about karma, it is the public enemy number 1 which frightens as much as the devil.

But karma is not a punishment. It is the soul's identity card in terms of experience and knowledge. Those who travel through the Akashic records will be able to confirm this. So why should we be content to believe that only fatalities pursue us?

The advantages are just as numerous as the disadvantages. From one existence to the next, we accumulate a great deal of potential skill, and this is what Gabriel is getting at. There must have been a time in your life when you felt immediately at ease without ever having learned a discipline. You may even have been praised by someone who told you that for a beginner you were very good.
Of course, the common thought is to brace yourself with an "I could never do that", so you were the first one surprised every time these facilities presented themselves to you. If you add up all the times you succeeded brilliantly in various fields without knowing anything about it beforehand, well...

"You can do what you don't know how to do yet!"

Despite the limiting belief, the unsuspected skills of your soul baggage emerge. This is manna from heaven to reveal and indicate that you are in

alignment with your Life Mission. In theory, you may not know how to change a car wheel, paint a picture, solve a complicated equation... but in another existence, your soul learned it and remembered it.
That' s the Divine Idea!
It's a combination of skill and intuition. At a particular time in your life, heaven will come to your aid to awaken your dormant potentials to serve your good and that of others.

Take the case of the great inventions that have contributed to the progress of our world. They were born from an “idea”. The people who had these “flashes of genius” were visionaries who chose to follow directions from elsewhere. Most of them were confronted by resistant spirits who tried to discourage them, but in their hearts, they knew, they persevered!
My mentor calls this phenomenon mediumship by inspiration, and he sums it up very well. When we talk about intuitive abilities, we always visualize the person who predicts the future, talks with the dead or handles energies. This mystical label does not

apply to everyone. From the painter to the doctor, through the diversity of talents that are on earth, all are mediums who ignore themselves!
They are divinely guided and assisted to put their natural predispositions into practice... And they excel in what they do! The Divine idea is surrender, the ultimate spiritual openness that nurtures self-confidence and individuality. All my life I've been blinded by the search for an impossible happiness. It depressed me when someone would say accusingly "You don't know!".

And yes, there are many things I don't know, and I'm not ashamed to admit it, but since I'm here to learn and the other person doesn't know everything either, we're equals! As the saying goes, we are all someone's fool!
However, what I know I can pass on and vice versa! If the sharing is done with respect and mutual richness, then it's perfect! I love to learn but because I was bad at school, I didn't understand some of my abilities and skills. I even tended to suppress them so as not to be seen as a "show-off".

Where did my resourcefulness come from? One day I asked my mentor about my "voice" and my psychic vision, and he replied: "there's nothing to understand, you have to be guided". I thought he was trying to get rid of me by cutting the conversation short, which made me even more defensive about certain aspects of my spirituality... Now I realize that he just wanted me to live my experience, because some miracles can only be lived from inside...

Coaching No. 6 - 6th letter

Awaken your latent potential...

"You can sing the song without ever having heard the lyrics..."

Archangel Gabriel - 2021

Gabriel puts his highest potential at your service in this part of the light coaching. His role is to awaken the divine idea in you. It is about putting into action the unconditional love of the source through the skills of the soul. It's about getting out of self-deprecation, understanding your talents and more…. This love will align you with your life plan and move mountains. I'm not talking about that ego-driven love that accentuates a sense of belonging or possession. The one I am referring to is a mixture of certainty, genuine joy and confidence that will move you forward with a light step despite the sometimes-unfavorable external circumstances. So far, the work has been on your inner sphere to counteract the cause-and-effect phenomena encountered in your life.

You will no longer be able to make mistakes because your choices will be based on the obvious. Like the previous exercise, this one is halfway between the spiritual and the earthly. It aims to prepare for a rearrangement of your life circumstances in order to enter manifested healing with Raphael.

You can do a preparatory exercise if you wish. It is to note in a notebook the circumstances in which you have demonstrated talents and skills that you did not think you were capable of.

This includes all the areas of your life where you have succeeded instinctively without having to go through any prior learning.
This list complements Michael's teaching *"By weighing, I restore equity"* (Michael is still working behind the scenes, don't forget that). It will help you put into perspective the successes you don't see.
To accept the idea that you are gifted and belong. Gabriel's strength will make your confidence grow and emerge. It is likely and even certain that additional talents will reveal themselves to you after the letter is written.

Sample letter

From:

Born:

"My Dear Archangel Gabriel, you told me: You know how to do what you don't know how to do yet!

I thank you for having put me on the way once again. Your guidance has opened my eyes to skills that I never thought I had. I was reminded of life circumstances in which I was able to ...

-

Explain the latent skills that surfaced and under what circumstances they were revealed

Gabriel, thank you for infusing me with your fertilizing power to activate my "Divine Idea".

May the innocence, joy, trust and love of the Highest surround me in a virtuous circle so that my latent abilities useful to the accomplishment of my Life Mission are reborn. I welcome and accept them with gratitude.

I am divinely guided; I am divinely gifted. I trust in you, in me, in us!

Thank you, thank you, thank you! I love you!"

This exercise will help you to discover and become aware of your divine magic, the magic that will never harm others and respects their life path.

It is the emergence of your truth, pure and clear. Give up control and move forward with a free mind. This magic will not enslave anyone because it will unite the spiritual parts of your being. You will be able to live according to the laws of your own free will because you are always guided to what is good for you. Social debts are settled, storms pass... Celebrate and honor your entry into a calm sea…

The Divine Mission

"If it sounds incredible, believe it! If it seems insurmountable, work around it! If you think you can't do it, look how far you've come! If it seems impossible, do it!"

Archangel Gabriel - 2021

From birth, each human being has a programmed of personal achievement that determines his or her major actions and accomplishments. The men and women who have left their mark on history led lives according to the customs of their respective times. Nothing seemed to predestine them to become "chosen ones". They themselves had no idea of the impact they would have on humanity. They were children, teenagers, adults...They loved, cried, laughed, suffered... They went through hardships before becoming role models for the collective consciousness. They made mistakes before taking a new direction...

But they did not anticipate the arrival of one of God's greatest ambassadors to proclaim the Word that would transform their lives!

The mission... the one these pioneering role models were destined for despite convention, they were the only ones who could do it!

The world's most inspirational figures did not take easy paths. The best example is Jesus, who faced the jealousy and stupidity of some men who were afraid of his influence.

He paid with his life for having opened people's consciences and encouraged them to see their environment with other eyes. In return, his faith was so immense that he made sacrifices to accomplish his mission on earth. This strength he possessed continues to this day, bringing light and comfort to all who wish to embrace it…

Daniel, Mohammed, Mary, Jesus and many others suffered many setbacks and misunderstandings before gathering followers. They did not know the outcome of events with certainty, but they moved forward with faith, convinced that they were being always guided and in their place.

Michael and Gabriel had been with me for several months already. In such a short time: My family relationships improved, I stopped losing money with my business, I was more focused, patient, motivated, full of energy, I started to know myself, I had determined what I wanted, what I didn't want anymore, my speech became more fluent, I wasn't worried about the future anymore.... I was happy... and I still am.

After experiencing all this, there was no looking back!

Why continue to suppress certain aspirations when life was opening its arms to me?

All this time I had simply been "surviving", trying to get through life as best I could. My chrysalis was cracking.

What to do? Where to go? I needed to do something that felt like me. I didn't care where it would take me, I wanted to live it with passion and enthusiasm. All the "no's" I'd come up against didn't matter anymore.

The mouths that had uttered those rejections had made the right choice; I didn't belong with them... As for those to whom I was used as a punching bag, I hope with all my heart that one day not so far away they will have the courage to let their light shine.

If Virgil helped Dante emerge from the underworld unscathed, I suppose my guides have been eager to hang up their wings and halos and move on to greener pastures. They have been patient, preferring to see me hopeless rather than destroyed...

The Archangels have been the heavy artillery that heaven has drawn for me to finally open my eyes. It doesn't matter where you are now. It doesn't matter if you are surrounded by two people or a million, you were born to fulfill a plan made especially for you. Can't you see it yet? Don't worry, it's about to happen!

Life has taught me not to always trust appearances. A big win, made of public recognition, means nothing about a person's true intimacy and way of life. Someone popular may be an emotional sponge who cannot find happiness, while an anonymous person may feel rich in every way. The focus should be on sustainability, not on ephemeral glories that last only a short time. The race for success and constant competitiveness are locks that prevent the project from being realized.

Today, it can be difficult to find one's mission. We're constantly exposed to ready-made products with which it is easy to identify temporarily. The good thing is that this brings out talents and passions, any inspiration is beneficial after all... But beware of imitators!

Following the wave of the trend by copying ideas or concepts to make a place for yourself is not necessarily the best method.

You will live in a permanent gap between what you do and what you are. You will believe it out of selfishness when your mission is perhaps elsewhere. If not, bright ideas may come to you.

You then talk about them with confidence and realize that others use them to their advantage. You may feel that your life is being stolen from you and that you are constantly being relegated to the background.

Don't worry, the success that is yours belongs to no one else. Sure, it's frustrating to see "opportunities" slip away, but are these opportunities a guarantee of a better life for you?

Look at all those actors whose visibility has exploded after playing an iconic role. Yet some were not the first choice to play the character that made them successful...

It was their mission and the circumstances aligned for them to succeed despite the opposition. Imitators have their limits, and they don't have your personal touch, the "divine idea" that lives only in you!

Beware of the double-edged sword of the life mission: confusing the call with an increased need for recognition! The need for recognition will bring you satisfaction while leaving in its wake the shadow of lack. From then on, you will immediately acknowledge that you have taken a circuitous route. The call will make you feel in perfect harmony despite opposition and possible obstacles.

You will meet people who will not understand your avant-gardism and will close doors to you. But you will also find golden people who will believe in your message and your ideas. Beyond that, enthusiasm will be your ally, your daily life will be made of colors despite some stormy days.

You will know exactly what to do at the right time, without worrying about the slightest result. And for good reason, you already carry success in your heart!

You will live in the world of certainties and with Gabriel by your side, no misinterpretation is possible! Rid yourself of the burden of an omnipresent popularity that tends to make you believe that without it you are nothing. The seed of the great man lies dormant in each of us...

Coaching No. 7 - 7th letter

Discover your Life Mission

"No storm will be able to stop you because you will then walk in HIS footsteps!"
Archangel Gabriel - 2021

It's never too late to reinvent yourself, to love, to act and to create. Your talent, your possibilities, your personality are eternal. Age and social status do not define the life you must lead. Behind the scenes, the best machinists are working to take you to the pinnacle of success.

This letter to Gabriel is the final step in his light coaching. This is it; you are finally entering into manifestation! This exercise is an immersion in pure intuition, your soul will totally express itself through you and direct the actions to be taken. Don't be afraid, it's so natural that you won't realize that you are acting without questioning. I was moved when this moment came, Gaby is very special to me and although he was never far away, I would miss him.

The voice of my conscience made me understand the pain my beautiful white angel and my luminous friends must have felt when I turned my back on them... I promised myself I would never let them down again.

The revelation of your Divine Mission with Gabriel will be between you and him.

You are beginning to reach a stage of understanding that will facilitate its interpretation. In any case, when "your announcement" is revealed to you, pay attention to the reactions of your body, it will speak for you. You will not resist; it will not seem impossible or far-fetched... You KNOW!

Gabriel is full of creativity, he can appear to you in dreams (day or night), send you repetitive signs, make your heart speak, provoke a chain of circumstances to attract your attention... Whatever the case, prepare yourself to live the most beautiful spiritual experience of your existence: the illumination that your soul is looking for so much.

Sample letter

From:

Born:

"My dear Archangel Gabriel,

My spiritual journey of these last months has been rich in revelations about myself. I can never thank you enough, you Divine Messenger, for taking me under your wing to initiate me to knowledge. Your teaching and revelations have led me to...

-

Summarize the discoveries and realizations that have taken place since the beginning of the light coaching.

-

Gabriel, my friend, the power of God, thank you for your intervention at my side. Thank you for revealing to me now my Life Mission, the one I am worthy of, and which will lead me to the place I must occupy. The Mission that will leave a lasting imprint of light and love in my life. The Mission that is in perfect harmony with my personality and my Divine Idea. For my good and the good of all. I have faith in your Word, in your light and in

the blessings that are foreseen for me, according to the divine plan. I accept and welcome my Mission with grace, and I commit myself to fulfil it with confidence.
I believe in you, in me, in us!
Thank you, thank you, thank you. I love you."

My sleep and my dreams served as a meeting point for the Archangels to transmit their messages. This is how Gabriel revealed "My Mission" to me.
I was surprised without really being surprised... The task seemed arduous and the workload colossal, but I was called by this long-suppressed desire...
My love for words and books was no secret to them. I've a boundless admiration for the authors, the thinkers who have been my refuge in my greatest moments of solitude. Writing is part of my work as a medium.
I usually write consultation reports for my clients, the words go away but the writing stays... Words are interpreted differently at different stages of our lives… Writing... It has made me live intensely but from there to tell my story... Would I go through with it? I had failed so many times!

I wasn’t in the resistance, but I wondered how I was going to bring my mission to life.

At the same time, I understood the reasons for my blockages with the spiritual world. I didn't escape the fashions and I was desperate to fit into the mold of mysticism. Except that it's not me! In retrospect, I am too rock'n'roll in my outlook to bend to imposed criteria.

I wanted to be free and help people free themselves, not keep them in fear as I had done all those years. I no longer needed maps, conflicting opinions, alarming verdicts, grandiloquent past lives to direct my life. I decided that I didn't want to do conventional clairvoyance and healing. If my abilities were to be deployed to help others, it would never be in the way I had approached it before!

I wanted to give love to the world to make it a better place! I wanted to offer people non-superstitious ways to improve their quality of life and reveal the treasures they hide within!

Welcoming the Archangels into my life has changed me completely. One should be able to ask them for help at any time to have the chance to experience bliss like mine! Happiness is a right that everyone should have in abundance!

My work base was established... I fell in love with my project, the baby would be born without fear interfering with its conception. My power to act was increased tenfold, what I was doing made sense... And maybe one day you will even read these lines, I don't know...

Discourage me? Never again, because the call was too strong not to answer it. Always remember that no man can oppose the perfect plan, it is within the reach of all! Then there will be no more elite, no more superiority... Only you and your unshakeable power!

When you know your Mission, don't ask if it makes sense. You will understand it when the time comes. Go where your heart leads you, be fluid as water and proudly proclaim "God is my strength" for He is the origin of all life. The ways of the Lord are inscrutable, those of Gabriel even more so... Discreet and subtle... like my dear Archangel!

Moment of gratitude

"Don't look for the best way to thanks others, start by thanking yourself!"

Archangel Gabriel - 2021

The work that awaits you next will take place in the company of Raphael. You will leave the inner spheres to learn how to manifest your potential in matter.

Before that, and to thank Gabriel for his teaching, it's essential that you take some time for yourself. Think of this time as a long weekend away from the everyday. I wrote him a letter "quartier libre" made of open-hearted confidences to show my gratitude.

I have started the ritual of giving him flowers every week. It beautifies my living room and feeds his lovely energy; I love to feel his presence...

On your side, I have no doubt that you will know how to thank him properly and fully appreciate his refinement. You will express your gratitude in the most appropriate way, you alone will decide how to pay tribute to the most wonderful of God's messengers. Let your little grain of madness shine through, the heavenly kingdom loves to see us innovate. If you continue to be guided, treasure the indications you receive, they are "bonus" healings that strengthen your armor of light.

Be content with being you and having faith...

CHAPTER 16

Body and Soul

Raphael - God Heals

"In the middle of the arid desert, a detail slows my crossing. At first, I thought it was a mirage, my vision blurred by the overwhelming heat. Yet it is real... Fragile, this young shoot of bright green contrasting with the gold of the sand...The seed has transformed the hostile environment into its natural habitat... Equal to itself, it hatches, becoming one with the wind of the divine... Raphael…"

Air - Heal and manifest

"So, God's breath passes through me to offer you the instantaneous blessing of renewed life."

Archangel Raphael – 2021

Air is the gaseous element that plays a vital and protective role, drawing its source from water. Its composition forms the atmosphere that surrounds our Earth, it filters solar radiation and regulates temperatures. A symbol of movement, it is close to fire, which it can feed, but it is also part of the triptych that seals life and makes it possible.
Air is an archetype of impermanence in its constant renewal, like the different stages of growth/ degeneration of the human body: birth, childhood, adolescence, adulthood, old age and death.
From a poetic point of view, the structure of the human being resembles the tree that has its origin in the earth. Water and air will allow it to grow, to expose itself to the light and become the most majestic of all.

Omnipresent, necessary for survival, impalpable and divine by nature, this element is the catalyst of the principle of manifestation. With its breath, it liberates, carries away, embraces, thus participating fully in the changes of cycles necessary for any accomplishment.

Water fertilizes and air ensures externalization in matter; it exerts pressure on any person with whom it comes into contact. From a scientific point of view, the ambient air is electrically neutral. However, it should be noted that the bodily effects it triggers according to the outside temperature are like the intuitive sensations provoked by our primitive instinct.

Spiritually, air can be seen as the intermediary element between the earth and the heavens. Our body is the receptacle of this vital substance, and through breathing we become one with it.

Of all our natural reflexes, inhalation and exhalation are the unconscious keys to understanding the phenomenon of resonance. The air flowing in and out of the lungs is like a boomerang, recalling a spiritual concept many of us know: the law of attraction.

Everything in our universe is energy! Like air, we cannot see it, but no one doubts its existence. When energy is used for a specific purpose, its flow is often interrupted by a parasitic and obstructive spirit.

On the other hand, no one over-intellectualizes the breath… Why should we, since air flows in abundance... It's obvious! Heal is to be certain that benevolent energies are naturally flowing in abundance to relieve our impermanent states. It is the alliance of earth, water and air.
The rapid impact force that guarantees regeneration and materialization. Cleanse and move on!

Raphael is the heavenly healer commissioned by God to restore all the ills of the earth. This dynamic Archangel can move with impressive speed to distribute his healing energy throughout the world. A true soothing balm for the heart, body and soul, his life-giving breath lovingly heals all who call upon him.
Raphael is also the protector of travel. His speed of action is uncommon, and he will oversee each individual journey and ensure that his protégés reach their destination. It is the companion of our evolutionary cycles, of our obligatory passages.
His ability to replace stagnant energies with impulses of vitality allows us to better understand

the vast skills he possesses to preserve and protect life. For it is in trial that we become aware of our strengths. Raphael is traditionally depicted with a green halo; his accessory is the caduceus which he holds up as a sign of healing.

In the mosaic in the church of St. John, Raphael holds a sword in his left hand and on his right a child is wrapped in one of his large wings. Over his immaculate robe, a garnet-red mantle symbolizes Noble Energy, serenity, truth and fidelity.

Such a contrast with the usual illustrations breaks with the classical patterns we are used to. Raphael conveys the robustness of the defender, reminiscent of Michael, the kindness of the benefactor like Gabriel and the comforting warmth of Uriel.

He embodies the quintessence of divine abundance, bringing us courage and fulfilment.

When Raphael manifests at my side, he surrounds me with a very high vibration.

I can clearly see streams of colored energy flowing through my hands and into my body. A miracle of regeneration!

As a healer, he is particularly sought after by those working in the field of physical and spiritual health. Some beliefs and convictions tend to reject medicine and rely on the will of the higher ones for survival.
It should be noted that every member of a medical team has answered the call to help others.
The long studies they have undergone to learn about the human body, its failings and how to care for it in all circumstances, are merely the guidance of Raphael who needs earthly emissaries to carry on his healing work.
The same is true of healers, who are interested in the subtle causes in order to treat 'evil' from another angle. Although there are different opinions on the subject, those who work to heal others are cogs in a well-oiled machine under the constant supervision of God's physician.
Instead of locking ourselves into hermetic visions, let us walk hand in hand, recognizing the limits of our skills and understandings so that we can pass the baton when necessary.
I really learned to use Raphael when I received my initiation as a healer. Unaware of the extent of his

energetic capacity, I preferred to avoid playing the sorcerer's apprentice by working directly with him for a client.

Wanting to do good does not mean being all powerful and doing anything. Being cautious, I first operated on my relatives and myself to get a first idea of the results I could expect to obtain.

I practiced on small wounds that were easy to treat: cuts, light burns, superficial wounds, menstrual pains... In spirituality, especially when it comes to healing, there is no room for failure or ego.

Getting a "small" result is a step forward to keep learning and challenging yourself, again and again...

There is no false modesty or excess humility in this way of thinking, it is simply a matter of seeing the situation.

The healer is not a "star", he is a giver and the person who comes to him is a receiver.

For the current to flow, it is necessary to accept the fact that a divine intermediary is interfering in the process by transmitting the force that will be most comfortable for both parties.

By doing this, the magic is free to flow where it will. Gradually, I felt comfortable enough to ask Raphael for help in healing people other than my own, but also for my animal friends.

I was eager to discover what Raphael wanted to teach me, it promised to be rewarding in every way. I encountered physical ailments that I was eager to resolve because I knew that their causes were psychosomatic in origin. Michel and Gabriel helped me to put words to these ailments, Raphael only had to operate to give me what I had to receive…

I get up every morning at 6am to drink a glass of warm water and go to the gym. This daily ritual keeps me fit and is my first moment of pleasure of the day. One morning, during my strength training session, I started to feel an excruciating belly pain. It came on suddenly and was so intense that I couldn't continue my workout. I managed to make it to the changing room to get my stuff, but I was walking half bent over. The gym is about 600m from my house, so the distance I had to walk seemed to be the longest of my life... When I got home, I went to lie down. I thought my stomach would explode because the pain was so great. I was completely curled up, my jaw clenched so as not to cry, when a wave of heat started to spread through my back and into my stomach.

My muscles relaxed progressively, I let myself be rocked by this beneficial energy which relieved me...

I had no notion of time; I was in total abandonment when the pain started to diminish…

At the same time, a lively voice came up from my entrails, I heard: *"Healing comes from forgiveness"*. Once, three times, ten times I heard this sentence which sounded like a mantra...

The heat in my back became more intense before going quickly up my spine, it was like an electric shock which made me jump. When I stood up, the pain in my stomach had completely disappeared...

So came Raphael's first teaching: from pain comes healing...

The power of forgiveness

Part 1

"Who do you forgive? To you, to the other, to the world's opinion? You don't really know..."
Archangel Raphael – 2021

As an act of unconditional love, forgiveness has great virtues. It's, however, one of the great challenges of life that we all face at one time or another. Forgiveness is one of the most complicated emotional aspects to put into practice daily. Trust is cultivated through contact with others, but unfortunately it happens (often) that souls with less pure intentions than ours use our unscrupulous kindness to play us...

From then on, anger, resentment, ruminations, wounds of self-love, abandonment and betrayal will progressively squat in the consciousness to silently eat away at the emotional and physical vitality.

The trap that everyone falls into is to put a band-aid on an offence. We are stronger than that, we don't care, life will take care of it... There is no shortage of excuses to make others believe that we take things with fair play!

At least, that's what we all want them to believe in order to have peace and to stop being seen as weak... Except that on the inside, it's not the same story... Of course, time takes its toll, but before that, in the head, it's Las Vegas... Neon lights, slot machines and open bar included!

Logic dictates that forgiveness means taking responsibility for an event that has caused us harm. It is common to repress one's own feelings in order to make the colossal effort of trying to see the other person as before. I see in my crystal ball the specters of misunderstanding already making their way, violently distilling a mixture of injustice and resentment.
In a way, the "damage" is already done, confidence is shaken, self-esteem is at a standstill!

Two options appear: Withdrawal, the shell is built, social contact is avoided by immersing oneself in activities that make you "forget".
Or you get drunk on encounters that are not destined to last since the alter egos, you find are vibrating on the same emotional level at the time. At the beginning it is comforting, the train of life starts again...
Except that the wound remains open, it oozes, and one often repeats the situation of departure, only the faces change…

I've asked myself about forgiveness many times. Along with love, these are two areas without a user guide. Yet they form an inseparable pair, but by experiencing them with ego one misses their deeper meaning. To forgive in an "earthly" way means to exhaust one's reserves of goodwill by doing violence to oneself.
Taking upon oneself shared wrongs, carrying the burdens of a guilt fabricated from scratch... Overall, one does not forgive for oneself, one forgives to reassure others of one's nobility of soul. The ground

is no longer just slippery, it becomes an icy, murderous slope...

I regularly walking on coals when it came to putting the subject of forgiveness into practice. I must have been an excellent nightclub bouncer in a previous life because I never forget an event or a face.

As a result, I have an annoying tendency to remember everything that has been done to me... In the smallest detail too!

Life automatically pushed me on the path of forgiveness except that I found myself in the same situation as with people: I didn't know how to go about it!

One of the values that drives me forward is *"don't do to others what you wouldn't like them to do to you"*.

I already get into people's lives by practicing clairvoyance, so I make it a point of honor to mind my own business in my private life.

Of course, since every action has an equal or opposite reaction, when they were handing out wounds to be forgiven, I chose the two worst ones: betrayal and injustice. I don't like to hurt others, so when I had to forgive, I would hide the pain by trying to put myself in the other person's shoes. This gave me peace of mind, and I was happy to be told *"you are so kind, so caring"*. Such compliments made it worth my while to suffer a little...

Except that the pressure cooker effect was already underway, and the resentment ended up taking up so much space that my desire to get the better of the other person was dangerously gaining the upper hand....

I launched into speeches full of incoherence where frustration and anger were mixed. My interlocutor, who had already moved on, would finish me off with a wave of his hand, and suddenly I became nasty and uninteresting... This is the characteristic of the egotistical human being, accusing his prey of toxicity to avoid looking at his own...

And I have experienced humiliations... I ended up feeling guilty and convinced that I had done wrong, that I had no regard for the sensitivity of the person in front of me... In the end, the knife was stuck between my shoulder blades, not in the back of the

person I was trying to spare… The pain I felt in my stomach was not insignificant, I am lucky to have a strong constitution and to be very rarely sick....
This episode was a wake-up call, I was so happy with my results with Michael and Gabriel that I thought I was off the hook for many things. This was clearly not Raphael's opinion... Learning from the best doesn't make you an expert, you just get wiser and wiser.

"Healing comes from forgiveness"

I realized that forgiving others is not as important as people would have us believe. We make forgiving our offenders a top priority, to feel better, because we must. It's a way of putting things right with society... But who really cares about what affects us, about this thorn planted so deep that it is complicated to remove.
To practice forgiveness intensely and actively must come from the ME devoid of anger and bitterness. One gives generously to others what one does not give to oneself. I had spent three quarters of my life betraying and denying myself, I was bathed in this

energy. Unconsciously I was attracting alter egos who felt the same discomfort as me.

To continue my transformation, I had to stop pretending to be a moral vigilante. What's done is done, there's no going back! After all, why try to dissect every word, every action or make snap judgments? Raphael's healing power deals with more than physical pain, which is only a signal that says a lot about our psyche…

Where Michael uproots by establishing detachment, Raphael will impregnate the body with his energetic fluids to heal the remaining gaps of these inner wounds. On the cross, Jesus spoke these words: *"Father, forgive them: they don't know what they do"*.

That says it all!

Forgiveness was neither in the hands of Jesus nor in those of his executioners. Raphael "God heals" is the referee sent to us to reset the score. Finally, to forgive is to be free from all constraints. It's a beautiful combination of detachment (from others and from oneself), intuition and alignment with divine magic...

Coaching No. 8 - 8th letter

Putting Divine Forgiveness in Action

"So, your heart is light, and you express compassion..."
Archangel Raphael - 2021

Earth accumulates, water fertilizes and air manifest. This chain of circumstances is balanced and creative when it is positive.

Negative emotions, on the other hand, activate the circuit in the opposite direction. Adversities make their way into the consciousness, which feeds them and then rejects them into your earth to accumulate as vitiated energetic deposits. At first, the body shows no visible impact of these repressed emotions.

But over time, a deluge of disturbing symptoms can appear and even threaten the quality of life. It would be tempting to skip the steps and ask Michael and

Raphael to join forces to release and heal in one step. But too much energy released suddenly could trigger physical reactions that could upset your balance.

Gabriel's intelligence intervenes between two active steps to drain the infection. Light coaching requires certain levels of understanding to ensure sustainability over time. Before learning to run, one must learn to walk. We are talking here about present wounds, active in this life. To succeed in forgiving implies to stop blocking on certain events. The precept of forgiving oneself at all costs leads to psychological pressure and a sense of failure.

Let us make a fresh start and be inspired by the words of Jesus on the cross. We agree that life is a constant impermanence; the soul is in tune with the world of light regarding its mission on earth. Here on earth, until understandings emerge, *"they don't know what they do"*.

This "THEY" includes the actors in the feature film we are currently playing. Jesus' call to God did not change the finality of his last moments, he had to

live them at all costs. It was when he came back to us that the die was cast. Jesus reappeared, without any rancor, continuing the Mission he had begun... He could have chosen to return, fists raised, ready to fight... No, he broke the codes, equal to himself, carried by forgiveness because he knew that the Father would always be with him.
He left those who persecuted him in their narrow-mindedness, so that they could understand for themselves. He never had to prove anything to them, he knew what he was doing!

Do you see what I'm getting at? We don't choose our forgiveness! Besides, nothing forces us to do so if the heart still bleeds. Heavenly arbitration is there to take care of that! Raphael, as a defender of life, will intervene in this sense.
The only obligation in this area is to find one's balance so that offence becomes strength. This eighth exercise, the first one that connects you to Raphael, will draw its inspiration from Jesus' *phrase "They don't know what they do".*

When we suffer an offence, it is a life test whose purpose is to highlight the degree of unconditional love we have for each other through the wounds of our souls. The mirror, the mirror again....
These trials are on our way to elevate us, to make us aware of our capacity to love ourselves. The oppressor sees the evils that we try to hide, but he also sees our light that he tries to diminish.

Why? Because he is not ready for evolution, so his vision pushes him to want everyone to be at the same stage as him. For the complexed person in a state of permanent insecurity, it's reassuring to have the upper hand over his "prey".
Now it's no longer a question of being slowed down in your Mission of Soul, you can no longer hold on to blocking sufferings but go with a light heart towards the best version of yourself. As each case is different, you are free to add whatever is important to you!

The main thing is to empty the overflow of feelings. Don't mentalize, your mind must be neutral.

Your aim is not to reproach but to get a sense of perspective. You take note of the facts that no longer belong to you in order to remove the scars.

You will prepare your letter based on the following points:

- Situations in your life that required forgiveness (forced or not)
- Your reactions to these situations
- The contexts that prevented forgiveness (judgements, resentments, ruminations, impossibility to express yourself…)
- The feelings, stagnant emotions, discomfort, physical pain that forgiveness/non-forgiveness caused.

Sample letter

From:

Born:

"My dear Archangel Raphael,

Divine Healer, healing breath of my body, heart and soul,

I call upon you in full awareness in the here and now to

benefit from your healing energy in the area of forgiveness. In my life I have faced...

-

-

Take stock of your life consciousness and your relationship to forgiveness

-

-

Thank you for flooding me with your healing energy that will put Divine Forgiveness into action. Thank you for letting all hurtful events, words and actions fly away into the light so that they transform into unconditional love that restores everything into energies perfectly in tune with my life mission. Nothing can stop me from moving forward, I am in peace with my life tests.

For my good and that of all. I heal through your light.

I trust in you, in me, in us!

Thank you, thank you, thank you!

I love you!"

The Power of Forgiveness - The Mirror Reflection

Part 2

"Everyone here is a treasure! You are worth more than the priceless because HE created you unique."
Archangel Raphael – 2021

Reaching the absolute is everyone's dream.
The reasons that encourage us to heal after a trauma are intimate, complex... We strive to create camouflages to jealously preserve these weaknesses to which we cling despite ourselves.
Forgiveness, usually centered on the emotional, is in fact multidimensional. The reflection of the mirror, that uncompromising and implacable prism, is a facet to work on for those who aspire to peace of mind.
There are no half measures when it comes to recovery. Generally, it is all or nothing. One is either preoccupied with the body, relegating psychology to the background, or personal development becomes

a fad and takes precedence over everything else. Differing opinions on the matter do not help.

Someone who takes care of his body is bound to be superficial and a spiritual person will be labelled if he takes care of his style. In the eyes of his fellow human beings, he will not be « real » because beauty is reflected from within, so it is incomprehensible to bother with trivialities like appearance. It's very difficult to situate oneself in these conditions...
We have seen how to approach forgiveness in our relationships, and we now know that in this area too, it takes the referees pulling the strings behind the scenes to give us what we are willing to receive. Completing the cycle of forgiveness includes our relationship with the body and all the destructive behaviors that go with it.

The first reflection of our image is in the eyes of others. This begins with the basic, silly and nasty judgments that automatically place us in the categories of beautiful or ugly. This is the way to enter the world: to end up branded like cattle to be sent to the slaughterhouse! To reach a certain degree of evolution means to get away from the judges and the toxic. Let them be what they are... They will get tired of it and go and spill their bile elsewhere!

In order to be accepted or at least to hope to live a quiet life, one uses the big means to meet the external expectations.

Clothes, hairstyle, make-up, plastic surgery, diets... The suit fits the wearer perfectly... So many injunctions that maintain lack and scarcity.

The reflection in the mirror becomes distorted.

The harmful spiral of the unattainable objective mercilessly sucks in the candidates who hope one day to cross an imaginary finishing line that would close this race to perfection!

Always more, pushing the limits, at all costs...

When your appearance and mentality change, you are proud of the new effect you have on others.

You never really let go because there's always someone there to remind you of what you once were... It's often said that the road to hell is paved with good intentions! The artificial light effect becomes a smoke screen.

So much effort for so little recognition in the end. The first defense reflex will not be to hate the perpetrators, the simplest option is to turn this hatred against oneself.

Compensatory reflexes set in control, addictions, disorders, excesses, destructive behaviors....

All pretexts are good to fill in the gaps, look for artificial paradises and punish oneself severely. A layer of varnish is applied to improve the visual, but the buried complex is always there...

Looking back on my life, I think that obesity was my problem to solve, and when I was given the incarnation challenges, I came across this one. Why did I do this? I don't know and I respect some of the mysteries. Now I know that if it is in my path, I can overcome it.

I am convinced that if we knew our life in advance in all its details, from our birth to our death, destiny would still have unexpected turns. Today I can say that I have no regrets about my past. Everything was beautifully in place; it just took me time to understand and live with it.

My excess weight was the cause of all kinds of ridicule. During my school years, some smart guys would poke my head in the toilet, and other days they innovated by sticking chewing gum in my hair. They pushed me ruthlessly to make me fall. Their delusion? to see if my fatness made me bounce... Brilliant... In their eyes I couldn't hurt myself. Their biggest blow was the day they wrote insults on my face in black marker...

I went to school anxiously, looking forward to the weekends. I was very lucky to be a teenager at a time when social networking was not yet a divine idea in the minds of its creators... Otherwise I think my misery would have continued outside school hours...

Weekends at home recharged my batteries, I was surrounded by my books, my records, my video games... I could sew, draw, create jewelry and many other things that I liked a lot…

I had great moments of silence, I kept almost everything to myself because I didn't know how to express what was happening to me, so I ate...
A bunch of idiots had decreed that I would always be the fat one and that no one would ever love me, so why should I care about my weight? I needed to hold on to life and my only light was food...

Today, what I experienced has a name: bullying! Unfortunately, at the time, it was called the school of life and getting through it meant having character, getting tough.
When I was 14, my mother came to see me one day in the kitchen. She told me bluntly that I had to go on a diet because my weight was a real problem. There weren't many plus-size clothes available in 1998, I was light years ahead of the models you see in VOGUE.
Her abrupt speech sounded like a punishment, but I complied. All I wanted was to be left alone and to stop being pointed at. Forcing things like this on me made me feel guilty, I felt dirty and disgusting in this body that I hated most of all!

I stuck with it and followed the diet that everyone wanted me to do. My appearance changed gradually but my mind was a minefield, if I put my foot in the wrong place it would go boom!

This race to look better lasted 20 years, I lost over 111 pounds in all. The miracle cure that was supposed to heal me gradually killed me.

My heart continued to beat, except that internally the gangrene spread to the slow agony that followed.

I developed eating disorders. I alternated between anorexia and bulimia. Eating became an ordeal, food was my number one enemy. I alternated between phases where I made myself vomit after emptying the cupboards and periods where I only drank water.

I felt a gaping hole in my stomach, a huge emptiness that I couldn't fill. I wouldn't wish it on anyone! I think the worst thing was the constant comments from outside. I had fought like a lion in the arena to earn the right to live, but I was never good enough, not cool enough!

I had compulsive eating habits, I smoked a lot too, believing that this would calm my raw nerves.
I bought clothes that I never wore. If they didn't fit, I was on the starting blocks for a new diet... I wasn't trying to feel beautiful; I was seeking to destroy me! I was a slave to a number on a tag so that I could finally hold up the banner of the perfect size and shout my revenge on life... I must have been stupid, naive or blind... Maybe all three!

At some point I just snapped! If there was one nightmare I wanted to get out of, it was this one! I experienced violence in words and deeds, I was abused, threatened, crushed, humiliated and I survived... Forgive them for they know not what they do... The downward spiral that was killing me slowly was my doing. That was the last straw! I was afraid that it was Michael who would confront me with my darkest side, but I was wrong...
The first stage of forgiveness went smoothly, Raphael was so effective that I didn't care about the people who had mistreated me. I just wanted them to be happy with people who were right for them.

All healing has its unpleasant ups and downs. I call it *"emptying the trash"*. As I approached this new coaching with Raphael, I was choking on the excess of emotions from this part of my personal history. However, it wasn't in my plans to stop… I had to keep my head high in the face of the emotional turmoil. I wrote spontaneously to Raphael about my relationship with my body.

I asked him: "Why did I do this to myself? Why did I let it happen?"

Here's his answer: *"The question is not why you damaged yourself but what pleasure did you get out of doing it. What you think are the good things, you use and abuse to hide the beauty of creation."*

I was shocked to see how right he was, again...

I had no control over anything because everything was imposed on me, my body was the ideal scapegoat.

A complacent and silent culprit that I could abuse as I pleased.

Playing with my life by experimenting extremes gave me a feeling of power that did not exist because the reality was quite different: I was being consumed from inside!

The puppet whose strings are pulled! This truth that I was trying to ignore jumped into view. I must stop burying my head in the sand and act.

Coaching No. 9 - 9th letter

Turn your addictions into light

"Don't battle against shadows, don't blame them, but understand them in order to tame them..."

Archangel Raphael - 2021

Maintaining your vehicle and taking care of your crew are the prerequisites for a smooth journey. Raphael, an experienced and caring captain, will help you make the necessary repairs so that your ship can go wherever it wants to go. The previous coaching dealt with the outer reflection of forgiveness.

By letting Raphael's energy heal the unfair situations that needed to be healed, you have completed the

consolidation of all the exercises you did with Michael on the roots anchored in your earth.
Now the healing work of the body and heart will amplify the benefits of Gabriel's actions on your ability to create in consciousness. The breath will stir up the remnants of stagnant water so that it becomes clear and limpid again.

When nature is unleashed, it is only to regain its rights later. She is stronger than those who try to oppress her, she makes her voice heard. Whatever he thinks, man is never the winner when faced with the revolts of Mother Earth.
He bends, he adapts but he does not dominate her because she imposes respect for her laws. Raphael will follow the same process during this coaching: sweeping away oppressions to establish the self-respect you deserve.

...What you think are the good things, you use and abuse to hide the beauty of creation...

You are perfect as you are!

If your soul has chosen the body in which it is now installed, it is perfectly suited to your journey. The embellishments and improvements you make during your lifetime must be suitable only for you. They will be the visual adaptations of your cycle changes, perfectly aligned with your radiance, your earthly, celestial origins and your attraction force. We never destroy ourselves willingly or for pleasure despite what we think.
Choosing to experiment is a fact but keeping the bad habits that come with it is reassuring.
Being conditioned by low self-esteem and the belief that "I'm not worth much" will let the consequences override the causes.
In 99% of cases, addictions, disorders and destructive habits are easy ways to escape from reality.

Food, alcohol, drugs, sex, gambling, escape from reality... just a few examples among the thousands of these false friends that control and amplify our malaise to better deceive us.
The work with Gabriel has made you aware of your natural talents. Your intuition is connected to the

Divine, the circumstances of your existence are beginning to reorganize. Old baggage is no longer necessary...

To go beyond forgiveness, the new energy that Raphael will deposit in you following the exercise will help you to measure the full extent of the path you have travelled in order to look at yourself with pride and love. In addition, it will act to rid you of all addictions that have taken control of you.

The subject of your letter is about demons that you know well, however identifying them in a preparatory note connects you to the energy of healing forgiveness. This is a powerful and symbolic action.

Here is a list of examples of topics that can be discussed:

- Physical addictions, controls and challenges to push the limits: cigarettes, drugs, alcohol, medication, food…
- Emotional addictions, another kind of harmful takeover in order to escape from an inconvenient reality: gambling activities, social networks, sex,

work, sport, appearance, emotional dependence, spiritual practice…

- Need for pain, self-injury (this includes all actions to hurt your body), devaluation, buried guilt

Be careful not to confuse the above-mentioned topics. I quote these examples which can be dangerous when they are based on suffering or trauma.
Then the actions are motivated by intentions that annihilate any good will.

To give you a situation that everyone knows: an angel and a little devil are on your shoulder, each one whispering advice in your ear. You feel lost but, in the end, you always listen the little devil even if you don't want to. It is in this light that we must consider the list of addictions that I cited.
From a healthy, moderate and balanced point of view no one will blame you for eating a good meal, smoking a cigarette or drinking a glass of wine, going to the gym to keep fit or enjoying what you do. If your actions are in line with your beliefs and resonate positively with you, you are free!

Sample letter

From:

Born:

"My dear Archangel Raphael,

I thank you for the healings that have already taken place in me in the area of forgiveness. Today I write to you to confide in you my addictions, my destructive attitudes of guilt that have made my body and my heart suffer....

-

Detail precisely what types of addictions and destructive attitudes have generated stress and trauma to the body

-

My dear Archangel, defender of life and healer of God, thank you for unfolding in me the energy of abundant forgiveness that will allow me to regain my self-esteem and experience unconditional love for who I am. May your healing power restore my body after all the abuse I have put it through. Addictions, destructive habits, guilt and unhealthy desires no longer have control over me. Guide me to a return to personal sovereignty and serenity of heart that will bring me contentment and acceptance of

my true inner and outer beauty. I have faith in your intervention and the beneficial consequences it will have on me. I forgive myself and love myself as I am. I am unique and in my place!
I have faith in you, in me, in us! Thank you, thank you, thank you! I love you!"

My problems had been going on for so long, I thought I would have to ask Raphael several times before I saw any results.
I underestimated him because the very next day I noticed a difference in the way I ate. I no longer felt the need to "fill up" on food. My episodes of food carnage stopped, and my cigarette consumption dropped dramatically. Now I eat healthily, little but well. My mother, who is an experienced cook, passed on her passion to me as a child, so I started cooking again. Raphaël has taught me to become an epicurean, I no longer try to destroy myself. Eating has become an act of love and sharing.
My gym sessions are more productive. I "feel" my body and I have discovered an endurance that I did not know I had.

I realized that I had made the mistake of losing weight for others, out of a need for recognition... Others did not try to change for me, and they don't have to!

My shape, my cellulite, my stretch marks... This body that has lived, these defects that I hated are gifts. I love it and I don't care if I don't correspond to totally bogus beauty criteria. A charisma is much more attractive than a perfect plastic!

My imperfections are part of my story and nothing in the world can change that. Never think that all is lost because Raphael can shine his light into the darkest corners of the physical and the psychic. No shadow can resist him! After death, resurrection...

Nature is full of extraordinary riches.

Everything is useful, perfect, aesthetic. One can see heights, curves, hills, defects, asymmetries that do not shock the eye. Depending on the location of the object of your observation, its apparent imperfections turn it into a unique wonder of the world...God did not create his earth to be perfect, he made it a work of art conducive to life...

Honor what you are and allow yourself to be reborn. You belong here, today more than ever!

Blessed relationships

"In every relationship, the positive is a glimpse of the ideal that awaits you and belongs to you…"
Archangel Raphael – 2021

The journey only makes sense when undertaken with reliable and solid companions. No matter how far we travel, this journey is punctuated by unexpected encounters that shape our story. Most of them are so important that they help shape us in some way. Meeting people again is an integral part of life. Even if we decide to go our own way, there is no enrichment without common interaction.

The fantasy of an ideal world is that we are only surrounded by "good" people. Persons with whom time passes quickly and who make us feel loved.

But since life is an equal mix of light and shadow, "bad" encounters are not easy to avoid.

Why do it after all? Those who have wronged us, whom we have permanently crossed off our road map, are far more useful than we think... And let's be honest, a universe of only people we complement would be an absolute bore. What else would we learn but what we already know? In a classic pattern, we look for people who fill in our gaps. In other words, who are supposed to give us what we don't have... Everyone makes this rookie mistake! We are convinced that we have nothing interesting to offer, except our affection and a few qualities that are difficult to recognize. As a good and desperate gambler, we bet everything on the other and cross our fingers to win the jackpot... Fortunately, that was before!

Today is a new day... Thank you Michael for freeing us from the original pressures (family, karmic, thought forms). Gabriel reconnected us to our innate potentials, which set the compass in motion again. Raphael, the Archangel of the heart who has been looking after our forgiveness, will now intervene in one of his favorite areas: the attraction force!

If we call upon him for healing, he is also known for his interventions in our social relationships.

Of course, there are angels who "specialize" in relationships (love, friendship, family), so let's be grateful for the incredible work they do. However, they will only deal with certain aspects of relationships. Because they master them, love them and above all are dedicated to their divine task. If we don't want things to get stuck, we need to take our demands to the top.

Raphael is the perfect intermediary for this. His healing powers restore attraction and abundance, and by extension, he will bring together souls who are ready to receive themselves for a specific time or for life.

When I speak of souls who are ready to receive, I mean souls who have already understood many of the lessons and who have shed illusory expectations. Healed souls, so to speak. They can work in pairs or groups to spread their light. They are ready for the common evolution; they vibrate on the same frequency and keep on evolving. It seems so simple... So why do some of our relationships not work the way we want them to?

The trap that is commonly set is to pretend to be ready, when in fact you are not.

It's a societal problem, there's such an atmosphere of competitiveness in the world that falling is almost unforgivable. As soon as you get up, you must whip the stallion back to full speed.

Sadness is interesting if it sells, in the short term of course, because once the hype dies down, a new drama takes center stage. Hiding the ordeal and pretending it never happened, accumulating phone numbers of people you never call, putting on a smiling face, conveying messages of toxic positivity.... So many ways of hiding from the truth...

Another worrying parasite: the perpetual search for soul mates, karmic relationships, twin flames...

I don't question soul ties because they explain a lot about our agreements and misunderstandings, I just deplore that all this is used as an excuse for our good and bad times.

Each relationship is unique and takes a particular turn but trying to analyze the reasons for our attachments feeds regrets and constantly questions.... I'm not saying that the search for truths is bad if it is done with an evolutionary purpose. What is interesting is to find a nuance in the tenacious belief of all or nothing. Spiritually, when we approach this kind of connection, we imagine a meeting of butterflies in the stomach and stars in the eyes.

If the experience goes wrong, it means there is a price to pay before the happiness we seek. Instinct then counts for nothing, and the ego blocks this wonderful connection that has suddenly gone haywire. We find it hard to let go of our loves.

And for good reason, not being free ourselves, it is difficult to conceive that the one we consider as an extension of the ego, can escape us...

We are never sure how many existences we have passed through. There have been a multitude of powerful connections, but that does not mean that they will be repeated every time.

There is an individual learning curve to consider, and these ideal souls may only have a short journey with us. Meanwhile, others we don't know who a better fit for us would be can't make it because we block the flow of life with obsessions... The attraction force suffers; it feeds on frustrations and disappointments, so automatically you have an idea of what is going on... Through relationships, the lessons of incarnation repeat themselves to bring us face to face with the truth: healing is no longer an option to be kept warm for later, it is a necessity!

When I think back on the relationship losses that have occurred in my life, I am glad they happened. Today, I find it hard to imagine being subjected to the kind of domineering temperaments I experienced then.

Those relationships, though disastrous, made me grow. And while I sometimes look back on them with a note of bitterness, positivity soon takes over. I prefer to focus on the qualities that these protagonists showed me before revealing the worst.

Let's be honest, without talking about responsibility, both parties at least encounter mutual misunderstandings. Of course, we must learn not to let ourselves be taken advantage of; it is out of the question to accept everything, because being burdened with reproaches is far from being a

pleasure. Spirituality teaches us to love our neighbor, except that in some cases it is better to avoid putting a blindfold on ourselves. You can't love everyone, but you can try to understand why.
Learning to defend yourself in case of an attack is natural. Without being selfish, thinking about yourself in a healthy way and setting limits for yourself already starts to change the attraction.
No, this will not create bad karma, rest assured! Trust your intuition, again and again. Taking care of yourself and being pleasant in all circumstances should not prevent you from having a say if you don't like something.

After all, some people we try to be accommodating with don't mind "throwing their truths in our faces". When you think about it, feelings are determined by intuition and soul experience, so instinct will always be stronger than anything else!
Listening to oneself can prevent many setbacks and ease inner conflicts. After the teachings of Michael and Gabriel, a first sorting out took place naturally in my relationships.

I stopped dwelling on everything that was wrong because it only blocked me!

Why waste energy on people who are out of my life and no longer think of me? Apart from subconsciously "reinforcing" them, establishing their dominance, that's all I was doing.

I felt more centered, I was in tune with my opinions, and I started to express them clearly. Some people realized that they would no longer have a hold on me and distanced themselves. The ties I had with those closest to me became stronger. Now I don't have many people around me, but we know that we can count on each other when we need them.

The forgiveness phase made me clear. I no longer saw the point of being accommodating and understanding when my instinct was to be wary.

I stopped feeling guilty for being myself, but I wondered how I could move up the ladder to improve my relationships significantly. I wrote to Raphael about this. I told him about the qualities I liked in certain people and the things that resonated against the good feeling I should have had.

In one of my dreams, I was transported to a crowded concert hall. I was sitting in the stands, the cheering crowd at one with the music, when I felt his presence beside me. His dazzling light was stronger than the spotlight on the stage. His healing aura could almost absorb me, silence replaced the noise and his advice emerged from the heart...

« The attraction only works halfway when the earth turns in the opposite direction. The world around you is built around this misalignment. Bringing in the Abundance of the Father begins with the souls he places in your path. Blessed is those who turn on the axis of the Whole. »

As I drank my coffee the next morning, a flash of light illuminated the kitchen wall and I thought of his beautiful words.

All my awareness's and understandings reached another dimension. Gravity is the force that holds us down. Our planet regularly undergoes energetic changes to which our bodies are supposed to adapt. But we have our own energy field. Depending on its radiation, the cohabitation between the earth's gravitational force and the individual gravitational force can be tricky. Attraction is not then about submitting an intention to the Divine and waiting for it to happen. Presented in this way, the mechanism is incomplete.

Our life and its "practical work" are an integral part of the earth's attraction. It's the place we were initially assigned at birth (family, place of residence, physical and social characteristics). It's temporary because everyone is destined to take flight. The earth turning in the opposite direction and the shifts are all roots and patterns that have been worked out with Michel: the initial place.

Gabriel and Raphael helped us to integrate the *Father's Abundance by placing us on the path*. That is, before attracting blessed souls, we first realign our own! We instill confidence in one's potential and abilities. The instinct of the heart guides our steps at every moment of the quest... *Turn into the axis of the whole*!

Following the path, finally going in the right direction even if it seems crazy! This is the secret of the attraction that works miracles: feet on the ground, head in the stars with a heart that connects the two worlds.

Coaching No. 10 & 11 - 10th and 11th letter

Restore relational attractiveness to its highest potential

"Become one with the world' s energy, then you will be home everywhere, you will not search anymore, you will find..."

Archangel Raphael – 2021

This stage of the light coaching has the particularity of being carried out in two parts. Two letters to write to Raphael so that his healing power converts your gravitational force, better known as the "law of attraction", into relational abundance.

It is about extending your personal magnetism to the world around you. Rather than repressing your charisma, you display it in full view.

The greatest books on the subject tell us that the brain is a magnet. So far so good, since the head is the part of the body that opens the channel to the higher planes. It is also said that our thoughts emit frequencies that send our directives to the universe. This is where the game gets complicated because to get results, it is advisable to have constant positive thoughts about the goal to be reached.

Except that controlling and directing your thoughts 24 hours a day is mental torture!

Let's be honest for a moment, experiencing various emotions or "low frequency" thoughts is a fact of life. Without being overly pessimistic, there are times when you don't feel well. The good news is that you are a normal human being and that's cool! Tipping into the negative from time to time is part of life. Wearing a mask of positivity if you don't feel like it makes you a slave. Remember that the best has fallen down many times before standing up with their heads held high! Stop having a complex about the excess positivity that is thrown in your face!

In France, we have an expression for strength based solely on outward appearance: *Le colosse aux pieds d'argile.*

In other words, behind a solid and indestructible exterior, at the first shock, the whole building collapses! To be aware of this is to feel much better and light as a feather.

If the brain is a magnet, what about the heart?

The mind can be confused, but the heart is never wrong! Moreover, this organ of love has its own neurological circuit. It transmits to the brain all our emotional data, those sensations that are at first impalpable, invisible... Like Raphael's healing energy!

The force of attraction works like an electric battery. It has two polarities: positive and negative. When it is connected in the wrong direction, the battery doesn't work. The heart/brain tandem is the battery that directs the energy in the right direction so that your attraction reaches its highest potential!

God said: *"Let there be light, and there was light"*. When the mind is short-circuited to the heart, attraction is at a standstill.

Ego and impatience push us to insist even though the heart tells us otherwise. We don't know what to decide, we are caught in the net of time...

Very common symptoms of dysfunctional circuits...

Beneficial events present themselves when we are ready to receive them, but before that we must accept the encounters that will make these opportunities appear.

Raphael will intervene to create a short circuit in your negative attraction. This represents your polluted air, the outdated patterns of the mind. He will then take charge of restoring your positive attraction force.

This is the healthy air, the materialization of the possibilities of the soul. This reactivation of the circuits will allow a fluid circulation of your attraction force.

I advise leaving an interval of 7 days between writing the two letters. The effects of these exercises are powerful, the energy will harmonize to create changes in the matter and in your habits. Dynamism and movement are on the agenda! It is therefore wise to give the body time to integrate the new functioning of its circuits.

Sample letter No. 10: Creating a short circuit in the negative pull

To do this exercise, the body of your letter should contain the following elements:

- Relationship patterns that you have repeated despite the warnings of the heart
- Instances of intentions you have set, or the result has been contrary to your expectations
- Your own repetitive thoughts
- People you felt compelled to be with when you didn't want to be
- The consequences of these relationships on your emotions

From:

Born:

"My dear Archangel Raphael,

I seek your help today in my process of healing the failures in my relational attraction. Over the course of my life, the voice of my heart became disconnected, allowing my mind to take over. This led me to experience these situations, emotions and relationships:

-

Explain the relational situations in relation to the elements mentioned in the previous paragraph.

-

Raphael, no one else is more qualified than you to re-establish the right current in my heart/brain connection. Thank you for healing the gaps that keep me in a negative attraction that no longer belongs to me. Thank you for establishing the equity of the powers of the heart to unite my heaven and earth in the positive principle of attraction that belongs to me by divine right.

I am a magnet for blessings, I attract blessed relationships, I attract positive circumstances into my life.

I trust in you, in me, in us, in my restored attraction force! Thank you, thank you, thank you! I love you!"

By wording your letter in this way, Raphael will stop the gears that block the arrival of satisfying relationships. You allow him to pour his healing flow onto you and positively reverse your pull.

By affirming that you are a blessing magnet, you acknowledge your sovereignty and leave the past behind. You are no longer the same person; you are entering a new part of your life. In consciousness you are ready to experience the unknown and all the opportunities it offers. It's a firm and definite commitment to your luck!

You believe in it, nothing can stand in your way, you will never run out of solutions and help.

Sample letter No. 11: Activating the force of positive attraction

When you love, when you feel happy, fulfilled, capable, beautiful, you notice that people come to you naturally. They smile at you, talk to you, give you compliments... The heart and the brain vibrate at the same frequency without being clouded by doubt. You are lucid, listening, in your place...

Your magnet is at its most powerful!

It automatically attracts, protects and keeps away toxic influences. Only the good wants to enter your life to help you continue your elevation to relational abundance. The purpose of this exercise with Raphael is to activate your attraction force at its highest level. The secret? Feel love, happiness and well-being in all circumstances.

The writing of your letter will be based on EVERYTHING that has helped you to evolve, on what you love, makes you happy, alive...

We focus on failures because our ego does not appreciate disappointment, however they are not most of a life compared to all those moments of small or big happiness that come to life in our sharing.

The key is to report the situations, emotions that have enriched you.

To create your letter, you can start your reflection based on these points:

- Positive developments/changes in your relationships

- What has this brought you? What did you get out of it that was beneficial?
- The inner and outer metamorphoses
- Areas where you feel free and happy
- Emotions you like to feel

From:

Born:

"My dear Archangel Raphael,

I seek your help today in my healing process. Your intervention on the failures keeping me in a negative force of attraction have been beneficial. In me and around me I have noticed these changes:

-

Explain the positive situations related to the elements mentioned in the previous paragraph.

-

Raphael, thank you for putting all your healing love energy into action to connect me to my positive attraction force. May the heart/brain connection be fully re-established, in respect of my Divinity. I accept myself with gratitude, I accept the blessed relationships that will complete my growth and evolution. I am free from the

past, only love lives in my heart. I am restored, in harmony with the world around me.
I manifest good and receive it in positive abundance. My relationships are love, sincerity, respect and harmonious exchange! I trust in you, in me, in us!
I am attraction, now and always!
Thank you, thank you, thank you! I love you!"

The feelings and manifestations that emerge will depend on personal sensitivities. Everyone will be able to appreciate the relational progress that will result from this. Reconciliations, decisive meetings, unexpected help...
Anything can happen! What happens will be totally beyond your control though! For example, if you are desperately waiting for a partner to return but he is not programmed to serve your greater good, he will not return... Keep your eyes open as Raphael will set in motion the ideal circumstances for you to get the perfect relationship for you.
Don't be in a wait-and-see mode, let yourself be surprised! The lights will turn green, and the obstacles will fall one after the other.

Personally, shyness has always been an obstacle. If I add to this my own experience, I almost became socially phobic. Talking to people made me anxious, caused me to have palpitations. After going through the two stages of coaching and writing the letters, I felt like I was on cloud nine.
Little by little, people started to stop me in the street to ask me for information, to talk to me... Very nice people started to come into my life. I received little attentions, help, smiles, words of encouragement...

What was a giant step forward in this area was that people no longer pointed out my faults or spared me their penny-pinching psychological analyses...
I was amazed to see such a breakthrough in my reality. Now I meet people who are positive, healthy and constructive. They are devoid of expectations because I have detached myself from the gaze of others, I take them as they are... For our common good!
Instead of going through complicated situations, I don't have to fight anymore. I don't have to ask for anything, what is useful to me comes my way before

I even have the idea. I am still amazed at how easy it is! I feel immense gratitude for my life, for what it is and what it brings me. It has meaning even though I don't know where it is taking me...

I just know that I am in the right place, and I take the opportunities that come my way, they are divinely orchestrated after all…

Divine Abundance

"Divine windfall is programmed into your soul from the beginning. Then the Father's abundance will come down to you on Earth…"

Archangel Raphael – 2021

Nature is rich in resources; each element has its own principle of abundance while living in harmony with the rest of creation.

The tree that produces beautiful fruit, the flowers that bloom in the sun, the plants and their magical properties... Just a few examples among many that show us the natural abundance that surrounds us.

Each element is in its place, taking advantage of what is given to it to develop as it wishes. Abundance is a Divine quality that everyone has without exception. Most beliefs limit abundance to the realm of money. It also applies to health, love, work and all the good things that life brings. Thinking of money first is not unhealthy, even if men have made it a symbol of power.

Having enough to pay your bills, fill your fridge, have a good home, treat yourself, spoil your loved ones, does not mean that you sell your soul to the devil. Let's not spit on money per se, but on our attitude towards it.

There is a big difference between not worrying about everyday life and spending too much to flaunt or to humiliate others!

Money is only one of the visible results of the abundance process. One of many... Life has so many possible manifestations that we cannot count them. But back to money, for it to flow freely in our lives, the current that directs our attraction force must function without short-circuit... To agree with us and then with others, an issue we worked on in the previous stages of coaching.

Do you understand now why money is not the vital emergency of the attraction force? Because in order to obtain a constant financial windfall, the value we attribute to ourselves must be in line with our future projections. Hence the importance of happily experiencing other types of abundance in order to obtain the material comfort we so desire.

I often hear people say, *"You attract to yourself what you are!"*. To illustrate these wise words, let's step outside of the framework of positive thinking that is useful to ensure the continuity of well-advanced personal work.

For this positivity to resonate, to radiate, to manifest itself in time and space, it's crucial to be certain of the energy that we send out. It's at this point that the re-establishment of the force of relational attraction takes on its full meaning.

Taking ownership of love, respect and forgiveness through heart alignment has swept away the unpleasant experiences. By extension, the positivity of our soul can be expressed without restraint. If mockery and conditioning buried me alive for a long time, the first breath of oxygen that came through my lungs when I resurfaced more than made up for the years of suffocation.

The enriching encounters that Raphael placed in my path, those people devoid of questionable intentions and judgements, proved to me how wrong I was to have thought so little of myself in the past. My earthly origins, my place in my family, my thought patterns, my failing divine masculine/feminine, the rejection of my intuition kept me in the belief that I was unfit to receive the finer things in life…

In my professional life, I worked hard but was not financially rewarded for my hard work.
Yet I invested time and energy... I felt guilty about giving myself the things I wanted, but I didn't skimp on the cost of pleasing others. I've put myself in financial danger on several occasions.
I sacrificed or postponed projects to favor those who came knocking at my door asking for help... In my

profession as a medium/healer, I was confronted with the belief that persists here in France, that a person who possesses abilities to help others should not be paid.... For a long time, I closed my eyes to this subject... Except that as a human being, I have bills to pay every month... To please others and try to earn a living in other ways, I had to do jobs I didn't like!

You don't tell a singer, an actor, a sportsman, a painter or any other talented worker that his or her skills should be made available for free to everyone! Yet these people attract crowds, touch people and give them pleasure through their creations. All work deserves to be paid!

Under these conditions, material abundance was unattainable. I was programmed in the wrong way...

Being kind, benevolent and generous does not prevent you from saying no when you don't feel like it. Thank you to these amazing, healthy and altruistic people I met for opening my eyes.

For a long time, I thought I was being taken advantage of, when in fact I was drawing on my own reserves of abundance to offer it prodigally to people who did not appreciate it! I didn't want to lock myself in an ivory tower anymore and was curious to learn more about "higher level" abundance. It had worked for me in relationships, I was much more socially fulfilled, so I wondered how I could extend it to all areas of my life.

By following the Archangels' coaching, I came out of my shell, and it brought me closer to others. I'm not a recluse anymore... I'm no longer afraid because I know that if I walk in the light, nothing bad can happen. I wrote to Raphael about this.

When I finished, I barely had time to put my pen down when I felt two strong waves of energy on either side of my temples.

It was as if two large hands had been placed there.

I closed my eyes, no more thoughts crossed my mind, the sensation was calm and restful.

I perceived wonderful colors, from a translucent green water to a darker green. I had a vision of a beach in the early morning hours, on a corner of the sand this message was written:

"HE has placed your wealth in the book of your soul. The abundance programmed for you is in the heart of the lines of destiny. Take it! And go ahead of the Almighty's blessings"

Did he mean that I should love the past part of my life? Was he talking about the hidden meaning of my destiny? About those wounds that now seem so far away? The answer was a big YES!

I had developed protective reflexes by letting myself be dragged through the mud, by taking refuge in silence and tears... I had fought battles that were not my own, out of devotion more than conviction... I gave without receiving or I received very little... But the lines of destiny were well drawn, because I was there... Against all odds!

I didn't fail, I learned resilience and value! Routine, boredom and missteps are my soul treasures understood and assimilated.

My actions didn't always produce ripe, juicy fruit, but I did get credit for doing something!

What I called failures were detours from my programmed abundance.

The book of my soul... in the heart of the lines of destiny...
I immediately made a list of my successes and those pseudo-failures that I had so cursed. I felt sure that the tide had turned for good with this discovery. I had not incarnated in the wrong existence, I just had to ingeniously use the threads that fate had woven around me!
With my eyes closed and my mind at rest, I said:

"I bless my life and its value…"

Coaching No. 12 - 12th letter

Self-worth and abundance

"The worth that you give yourself is the measure of your cornucopia…"
Archangel Raphael – 2021

The final exercise of Raphael's light coaching will set the energies into action so that you and your Divine abundance can be reunited. This moment represents the material realization of all that you have been working on so far:

- Releasing and detaching (Michael)
- Feeling and knowing (Gabriel)
- Healing and recognizing (Raphael)

Before shining and rising with Uriel…

Our personal journeys lead us to believe that abundance belongs only to others.
What our earthly minds call luck for some is merely an expression of divine abundance in a specific situation. These "lucky ones" are a little more aligned with aspects of their life mission than the average person, which explains their success!
From a practical point of view, we saw in the section on Michael that we rely on what exists, what is anchored: the projections that are sent back to us. When charitable souls who slowly disperse their venom to keep us from shining, disrupt the hard-won bits of self-confidence....

You have reached a level of understanding that allows you to see the other side of this distorted picture: the divine reality that is quite different. There is a plan for everyone, and to achieve it you are aware that your soul has many tools at its disposal. Abundance is one of them!

Everything you envision, dreams, plans, desires... These things that are important to you point to your divine abundance. Before we see it manifest in our environment, we must feel it, live it in every moment: *HE has placed your wealth in the book of your soul...*

Raphaël wants to talk about value, the value you give yourself, that has no price, that priceless treasure that is only waiting for you to realize it. Your gestures, your voice, your smile, your personality, your character, your sensitivity, your energy... it is this abundance that makes you unique in the book of your soul. How can you attract the best if you feel you are not up to it? You can't do wonders with the belief that you are worthless and that you don't do anything well.

The letter you are about to write to Raphael finalizes the healing of the last inner wounds by reintegrating personal value into your programming. The value you give yourself is the secret mechanism of Divine Abundance.

Become one with your personal treasure and it will emerge as gold in reality... Preparatory notes are imperative for this exercise. You will need to make a chart in which you note all your successes and failures without exception. Don't give in to the temptation to count the number of successes and the number of mistakes, we are not interested! We are not interested in quantifying but in understanding! Don't cheat either, Raphael already knows what is true or false so don't try to hide anything!

- In the **"Success"** section, you will see all the similarities that emerge. There are always similarities in every success, the basis of your value, the parts of abundance that you naturally live with without question.
- In the case of **"Fails"**, you will also study the situations that have similarities between them. Revealing what went wrong in these cases

highlights the value you are denying (through judgements, self-sabotage...).

And here, Raphael will put all his talent at your service. His healing energy will act in superposition…
With the power of Michael: The Prince of Hosts has freed you from the earthly roots, the breath of the divine healer will fill the remaining gaps in your body and your memories of the traces of diseases, traumas, bad values....
To the life force of Gabriel: The messenger of God has awakened your buried potential to show you the way. The protector of life will multiply your positive values to program you to your personal successes.

... The abundance programmed for you lies at the heart of the lines of destiny. Take it! And go before the blessings of the Almighty.

Sample letter

From:

Born:

"My dear Archangel Raphael,

You, the wonderful divine healer, I call upon your wisdom and healing energy to multiply my awareness of my worth today. This is the key to my divine abundance, the value manifested and materialized in my dimension. By analyzing my successes and failures, I have understood what are the strengths and weaknesses that keep me from living all the forms of positive abundance that are intended for me:

Explain the positive and negative values that you have discovered by examining your successes and failures.

-

Raphael, thank you for revealing my self-worth in its full unity. I confidently express it without complexes and manifest in my life, in matter, the positive abundance in everything. Thank you for proceeding to the complete healing of old wounds, my lacks are divine abundance. I am fulfilled in ease. Understanding, full awareness and joy accompany me in the realization of the Idea and Mission that are mine and more! I am abundance, I am worth, I am wealth. I trust in you, in me, in us! I am invaluable! Thank you, thank you, thank you! I love you!"

What happens next?
The magic of life will begin, I have no doubt that you will find an incredible inner goldmine that will make you rich and abundant on many levels.

For me, I have continued to experience major breakthroughs in my evolution. The analysis of my successes and failures allowed me to clearly discern which situations were not for me, what I could do and what I couldn't do. This helped me to create a more pleasant environment and I started to manifest abundance by focusing on areas close to my successes. I no longer had to force myself or try to prove my worth to anyone as I instinctively went in the direction of my heart. In my reality, I saw a meteoric transformation of my destiny. Acting in accordance with my value has attracted opportunities I never expected before.

I have noticed that I'm less of an emotional sponge. People come to me more easily, my sensitivity and empathy are balanced, less emotionally dependent. Naturally, I don't let myself be intruded upon anymore, my exchanges with others are interesting...

The expression of these few results may seem insignificant, but Raphael was right. As soon as we accept the fact that we carry divine abundance within us, our actions attract equal and even better reactions!

...And go before the blessings of the Almighty…

Moment of Gratitude

"The way you take care of yourself defines the way you take care of others. Listening and recognizing your needs sustains my healing energy..."
Archangel Raphael - 2021

You're almost at the top of the staircase of the coaching of light. The final step you will need to take is to push open the door to Uriel's realm.
But before you learn to turn each day into a victory, take time to adjust to the major changes that have occurred as a result of Raphael's healings.
When I reached this level, I wrote a letter of gratitude including Michael and Gabriel.
As the energies of the three Archangels came together during the Divine Abundance work, I wanted to renew my gratitude for the blessings and teaching they had given me.

"My voice", which has now found its rightful place in my life, suggested I write an affirmation on a piece of paper. I carried it with me for seven days.

I then put it in the envelope dedicated to my correspondence with Raphael. You can do the same if you wish or adapt it according to your beliefs and feelings.

Here's what I wrote:

"My dear Archangel Raphael,

Thank you for the fantastic healing waves you have placed in me. The gratitude I feel for Michael, Gabriel and you is infinite. I am grateful for the healing and manifestations that have occurred in my life as a result of the exceptional work we have done together. Thank you for restoring the goodness, trust, faith and abundance that I now affirm and experience every day with myself and others. My life is a miracle always manifested. Thank you, thank you, thank you! I trust in you, in me, in us! I am truth, I am always moving on the right path!

With all my love and gratitude!"

To complement this, I focused my daily exercises on stretching to coordinate my earth/sky connection and gave myself a massage to release any tension in the body. Taking care of myself was an act of faith in my newly restored divine abundance.

Any physical or spiritual work, which is very positive for the soul and consciousness, requires care afterwards to help the body release the pressure and experience the changes intensely.

This is the stage of reintegration, the body vibrates, moves, is in the center of the energy axis.

The transformation is now successful. Your own worth is established, the shadow will no longer be able to reach you.

You can integrate your chosen wellness routine into your monthly activities and, over time, try others.

Be daring, let yourself be attracted by activities that appeal to you and that you have never dared to try.

Start to rekindle your sacred flame... Trust Raphaël, he will give you the steps to follow to pamper you properly!

CHAPTER 17

From Lead to Gold

Uriel - The Flame of God

"In the shadow of an endless night, the hermit advances slowly. His body, enveloped by the surrounding darkness, melts into the blackness of the setting. From place to place, he has walked without finding it, driven by the quest for this golden glow...Vivid, fleeting, it appeared to him at the turn of a dream... During this journey to the ends of the world, he carries his goal as his only luggage.

His gaze eventually became accustomed to the darkness, instinctively he could feel the unevenness of the earth his feet were treading on...

Suddenly, in the distance, the unexpected... The sphere irradiates the pupils that have become almost blind... The hermit is attracted by this light that he has struggled so hard to find... He approaches it, with a festive heart and a mind clouded by doubt. And if it still escaped him? But she is there!

Warm, vibrant, taking on an incredible size as he approaches it... He finally reaches her, and she sucks him in with her rays...

A new day dawns, illuminating the beauties of the world to the one who has sought them so much... He who walked the road of truth was worthy to know his name... Uriel…"

Fire - Illuminate and radiate victory

"Winning, losing... That is not the outcome, only life in its perfect expression is important…"

Archangel Uriel – 2021

Light and warmth are the major assets of the last element we will discuss. Of all the elements, fire is the only one that has been domesticated by humans, who have learned to light and maintain it as part of their daily lives.

Its use by primitive peoples brought about a major transformation in ways of life, marking a new turning point in human evolution. In its natural state, fire originated in lightning and volcanoes.

But long before that, billions of years ago, our Earth was a molten ball unsuitable for life.

This is very evocative of the changing nature of fire: impulsive because it never really dies, the flames being allowed to survive under the ashes...

Fascinating, it enlightens, protects and purifies but beware of its destructive side. The control that one exercises over fire is only illusory, it will die out, become dormant, give the impression of having been dominated... But watch out, because its revival phases are merciless!

The consequences can be terrible when he destroys everything in his path. An unstable element, its outbursts are however temporary, unlike earth, water and wind, which must be avoided and adapted to in the event of a disaster. But let us not misunderstand the power of fire.

It's tempting to make comparisons between the elements and relegate it to a "secondary" place.

Yet they all work together and complement each other at the right time.

- The earth carries fire within it (its primary origin, the magma of volcanoes) and fire increases its temperature.
- The wind feeds the fire. It stimulates it, spreads it, but in a restricted space and deprived of oxygen, it dies.
- Water extinguishes fire, but on the other hand fire can heat water or melt ice.

As the keystone of any initiation ritual, the vibrant light of fire keeps shadows at bay. It becomes the expanding force that must be nurtured to fully blossom... Just like us!

It's not surprising that the divine secret of fire has always fascinated man. Its flames are the material aspect of the reactions, feelings and emotions that inhabit us. Attracting or rejecting, the best and the worst, what makes us proud or ashamed... The existence fully lived, with its victories and debacles.

It is the demonstration of a passionate, vibrant life, radiating splendor!

Usually referred as the first element, fire here closes the last stage of light coaching with Uriel, the Flame of God. Considered as a less powerful Archangel compared to his acolytes Michael, Gabriel and Raphael, he is nevertheless the golden ray that illuminates us at every moment. His main attribute is to carry the torch of multidimensional knowledge.

Uriel stimulates mind, instructs and protects, nurturing the sacred fire of the soul to ultimate fulfilment. His sweet energy has the particularity of accumulating celestial light to spread its brilliance on the earth.
A true rejuvenation cure!
Archangel of joy and vitality, Uriel is an inspirational figure. A divine muse who attracts the eye and gives the work its singularity. Without him, the melody of life is incomplete, he takes care of the arrangements and the rhythm.
He is the warmth we so desperately need at the dawn of a new day. Uriel's aura as an artist is magnetic. On the great dance floor of life, he masters the choreography and encourages the shy to sway until the end of the night. He has Gabriel's refinement in

him. In creative matters, their functions complement each other because they are both messengers. Gabriel is the introverted intellectual who deals with the inner spheres. Uriel has the audacity of the extrovert, always having a Plan B in reserve.
Gabriel announces the crucial steps, what cannot be changed, the plan of life decided by God.
Uriel, through the knowledge and enthusiasm he imparts, feeds the Divine Idea by providing the inspiration and motivation to make the Mission ahead a reality. He teaches us to transcend the past and not to be ashamed of it, for whatever happens, we must live with it.

At this level, Uriel acts positively in understanding our knowledge, skills and ideas so that we can transfer and use them in our life cycles. If we wanted to generalize his intervention, he puts the best immediate potentials at our service. I'm talking about quick thinking, quick decision making, quick to channel information, quick to respond... In short, it conveys charisma and intelligence! This is the free and natural side of fire, the Flame of God, the

beauty of the soul that is unique to each being, that fervor that nothing and nobody can extinguish! As we'd say in France: *"C'est de la bombe bébé!"*.
It was Uriel who gave me the green light for the teaching I was to receive. Remember, he showed me the hourglass and the key on his first visit.

My teaching time was almost up, I would soon be able to open the doors that lay before me...
Uriel... extravagant, unpredictable, colorful. His cheerfulness is contagious, and I was very happy to see him again after all these months spent in the archangelic energy. He was no stranger to the beginning of my externalization. From the sidelines he was sending me joyful shocks to facilitate the integration of the lessons I was receiving; I felt it and I was sure of it! He turned up again on a beautiful spring morning. I was still expressing my gratitude to Raphael when on the third day Uriel appeared.

The event he materialized in my life that morning was totally unexpected and if I had known about it beforehand, I would not have believed it...

So unexpected... Fortunately, we don't have any control over divine synchronicities as they always work out for our good.

In 2019, I experienced heartbreak and the worst betrayal of friendship simultaneously.
There was W. an artist, shy, charismatic, spiritual...
And in his entourage, T. who struggled to impose her supremacy, consumed by an inferiority complex matched only by her cunning.
I thought I had found friends, real friends. You know, those exceptional people you want to keep close to you forever. Reality would later teach me that I landed in the worst of all crab baskets!
I liked W a lot. He emanated an Olympian calm and an apparent serenity that I sorely lacked. God only knows the storms he had to face... I felt such tenderness for him that I imagined I felt true love!

Life's experiences sometimes make us a bit stupid, especially when the heart gets involved... And I should have learned to hold my tongue... I imagined that T. was my friend, and nothing could have made me think otherwise. Her poorly channeled authority made her look like a madam reigning supreme in her brothel. Despite this mania for wanting to control everything in her and her little world, she was a nice person... I thought so, at least!

Looking back, I know that false friendships exist and that some people go to superhuman lengths to put up with us while putting on a happy face... Jealousy, secret hatred, envy...

I don't know the motives of these people and it's better for me never to know, the main thing is to heal the scar that the knife left in the back... T. must have felt that way about me, because she didn't go easy on me when she stuck the knife in...

One day I dared to declare my feelings to W.

I did it in writing, because that's how I express myself best. My shyness would have made me stammer... Of course, he didn't reply to what I wrote to him. His silence spoke volumes... I didn't try to contact him again and I was ashamed of opening my heart to him… Then, three months later, four

days before my birthday, he wrote back... And not in the most delicate way... Just an email, cold as ice...
T. the "loyal friend", the one I trusted and talked about my feelings for W. knew that I had been brutally dumped by email while I kept my pain to myself.
As a true strategist, she played the sympathetic friend in front of me and took care of breaking me down with W. from behind. She was the one who told him to send me an email, she even helped him to write it... Let's salute the extent of the vice!

I cut off all contact a long time ago, all that is behind me now. That rejection was finally a blessing in disguise, I was done with it... With time, you get over everything... Except Uriel didn't think so...
Let's get back to the present time, to that famous morning that would officially bring me into the final line of the Archangels' light coaching.

I've become an adept at preparing healthy meals and for one of my recipes I was missing a few ingredients. I'm lucky enough to live in the center of

Paris, in a neighborhood with all the amenities, including a supermarket 2 minutes away. No question of being lazy, I took a break from my cooking schedule to go and get what I needed.
I'm used to doing my shopping in "relaxed mode", which means jogging, without make-up or brushing. For this type of outing, I don't see the point of dressing up in my best clothes.... Except on that day!
I was about to go out wearing leggings and a sweatshirt with the inscription "All I want for Christmas is...", so my seduction capital was at a very high level with this kind of outfit, when I heard *"Make yourself pretty"*.
Always listen to instructions, even if they seem crazy. God's messengers are always right!
Despite my monumental laziness, I put on a proper outfit. With music blaring in my ears, I run out of my house down the stairs as usual.

On the street, I'm heading towards the supermarket when a male figure arrives in front of me. The heart of Paris is bustling with life, and passing people is part of everyday life.

Except that the figure in question approaches and stops... W.!
I hadn't seen him for three years... Yet he works a few blocks from me so the chances of running into him were more than enormous. The course of events doesn't always go the way you expect at the time. There is a Divine Timing to everything...

He looked surprised to see me, his eyes widened, and I think he thought I was going to stop and talk to him. To my astonishment, I didn't recognize him right away. In the past, I have dreamed a thousand times about this moment, building in my head different scenarios of how I would react... And there, nothing!
My heart didn't go boom, I wasn't angry, I didn't even think about the pain I felt in the past.
I just wished with all my heart that he would find the inner peace and happiness he deserved...
I continued walking, filled with an immense sense of liberation.
I was healed of him, of this man who was a symbol of impossible loves that didn't correspond to me.

He seemed surprised that I was ignoring him... This is the characteristic of people who evolve slowly, they imagine themselves so unforgettable that they believe yesterday's feelings remain relevant in the present... Classic trap of ego's silliness!

I also thought of T., the one who thought she was strong by betraying me... I didn't blame her; she was blinded by her own suffering... There are reasons for everything and if I had any lessons to learn, some people use their troubles as outlets for grief. The energetic boomerang, the badly directed fire, still and always a mystery of existence that we will never stop trying to elucidate...
Love is not about using the other person as an excuse to cover up your shortcomings.
Love is about moving forward together to grow and complement each other. Two souls bonding to grow their individual light with tenderness and respect.
This betrayal and rejection were a revelation.
Hypocritical relationships, never again!

Living in domination, illusion... I will have ensured the continuity of all that I had already experienced emotionally and socially!
My luminous team saved me from a monumental setback. I wandered aimlessly through the aisles of the supermarket, almost forgetting what I had come for... I heard a crystalline laugh and *"See, I told you to look good!"* Uriel has an undeniable talent to downplay things...

Uriel, my light... I don't think his goal was for me to prove to W. what he didn't even bother to earn. Evolution is not a race, and we are often confronted with morons who think they have done better...
No, I know Uriel saw how many tears I shed in this story, and he only wanted me to feel equal, in harmony, not inferior…
With this meeting, I was turning the page on this unfinished experience. I had become lucid and independent enough to no longer accept this kind of situation. My worth was restored to perfection!
Later that day, Uriel visited me again. I was writing down my impressions of the chance meeting in the

morning, with coffee and music in the background and a happy mood. The next song on my random playlist begins, a blinding flash of light filled the room.

As the Queen of Soul sang, Uriel arrived. I almost wished he'd taken my hand and asked me to dance... Let's get serious! Instead of dancing, I was going to get his valuable advice and listen to a lot of disco. Nice program in view!

"Strip yourself, clothe yourself in the fire of the Father, then the light will no longer stand out in the eyes of the world. Join the joyful Faith of the Kingdom of Heaven, it is waiting for you…"

He stayed with me until the song ends. I think he didn't want to leave me alone so that his energy would help me integrate his message.

... Join the joyful Faith of the Kingdom of Heaven, it is waiting for you...

Was I going to take the leap of faith?

The completion of our advancement with Uriel symbolizes the realization of all the personal work done so far.

The new base energy, the return to the origins of light. This green plain, once again, is none other than the land that Michael has conscientiously tilled. The yearning to explore uncharted landscapes was, until recently, Gabriel's fertile source.

The dazzling manifestation was born from Raphael's healing breath... Joy, happiness, love... The kingdom of eternal life... Spread, share, be free... The phoenix rises from his ashes...

The inspiring light

"HE shared his wealth with the world HE created, and his children will do the same!"

Archangel Uriel – 2021

The psychological aspect that raises the most questions when working on oneself concerns the radiation that

one emits. Becoming more conscious, succeeding in accepting our life and seeing it in its best light completely transforms the energy that emanates from us.
The old things are gone, nothing will ever be the same again. We finish writing one chapter of the book to start the next!

As with any change, there is a period of adjustment before taking new bearings. As peace is made, as we feel empowered, as we are in good standing with ourselves and as the opportunities are now unlimited, there is a small period of latency where we wonder how we are going to put our new abilities into action.
Desires, projects, ideas, motivation is at its peak, the machine is thriving. It's a bit like moving into a new house.
We like this new place, the rooms and walls are neutral, we visualize the future decoration but now the boxes are piling up and projecting ourselves on the result seems uncertain. But this home is the cocoon that will host the wonderful moments that are on

the horizon, so you must add your personal and creative touch. Giving yourself a break is a normal reaction!

Depending on one's ability to adapt, establishing new habits takes time. Indeed, this short-lived slowdown is a sign that the flight continues.

We are always encouraged to fight, to excel. Whether you are a seeker of truth, seriously ill, desperate, overwhelmed by problems, seeking wellness or otherwise challenged by fate, the pattern is always the same: you decide to take the path to recovery!

Making things right or getting better becomes the number one goal. When a breakthrough occurs, we are happy to see the light at the end of the tunnel. At the same time, we make plans, but they still seem far away.

Once you are out of the rut, once the chains are broken, once the ashes of the nightmare are scattered in the garden of memory, the integration of a new reality is just as disturbing as the problem-solving phase. Why is this? Because we are used to the effort and the fatalities that fall upon us. It becomes almost a safe environment that pushes us to our own limits and at the end of the fight we proudly declare *"I conquered"*.

The little detail we don't see is that a challenge has presented itself and we have chosen to look it straight in the eye. Victory over restlessness, the demon defeated... Believing ourselves capable of nothing when we are capable of everything!
Despite these mountains being moved, our faithful friend the ego has difficulty accepting to be put in the wardrobe.
This capricious one starts its deviousness again by creating the fear that everything will start again, and that happiness will be short-lived... Where is the savior? Here, in front of us, in the mirror!

By deactivating most of the limiting mechanisms, we can understand that these "fears" are not real... The men and women of yesterday are not the men and women of today, let alone tomorrow. Let the sunshine in... My chance meeting with W. was a very beneficial shock to my conscience and my soul.

When he rejected me, I had decided to close my heart forever, calling love dangerous. All the wonderful exchanges I had with my charming Archangels made me understand and integrate that I always loved love, I couldn't see myself depriving myself of the most beautiful feeling that one can experience in a human life.

Without love, my time on earth is meaningless and seeing it again confirmed that I no longer felt the desire to dwell on the past and the actors who played a part in it. The transfer of power between Raphael and Uriel was the point of impact that proved to me that I had chosen the path that was best for me. I have a life full of beautiful projects and I'm happy to get up every day to make them happen. My heart and my head are in tune, my decisions are in phase... Now I don't hesitate, I go for it!

Strip yourself…

This meeting with W. had to take place... under these circumstances and not otherwise! Yet he and I did not exchange a single word, but it was the ultimate concretization of all that I had experienced with the Archangels. My change was not self-suggestion, together we had acted, for my own good and everyone else's! Stripping off meant completing the complete work of detaching myself from everything that made me suffer. I passed the test of fire; its destructive aspect was divinely controlled.

Clothe yourself with the Fire of the Father...

The day after Uriel's visit, my body began to function in slow motion. It seemed that all strength was leaving me, morally I had ups and downs. I was torn between the certainty that my new plans would work and an old fear that I would find myself on a slippery slope again.

The sneaky ego, again... By provoking an upwelling of unpleasant memories, it hoped I would doubt all my progress. It cannot be said enough, intense energy work on behaviors and habits must be fully integrated to be understood. This face to face with the shadow is essential for the new radiance to flourish, it is part of the contract, whether we like it or not!

We must raise the sails and hold the helm firmly so that the wave does not swallow us up. We change sides, initially we were in the place of evil, agitated by Michael's domination. Now we hold the sword firmly in our hands!
The ultimate test of light coaching! Uriel certainly wanted to know how I would handle this temporary crisis... What would be my choice? Blind faith or reassuring fear? Clearly, my final lessons were going to be accelerated. So, I wrote a letter to Uriel confiding in him what my ego was doing to me and how it thought I could *"adorn myself with the fire of the Father"*. I felt the energy stirring in my solar plexus. I felt as if a bright star was living inside me. Like a sacred song, Uriel's words burst into my heart:
"The inspiring light is the spear of faith that pierces the devil on earth. He who wields it wisely will have access to knowledge, then the fire of the father will burn in him for eternity."

Uriel's intelligence is impressive, and not having enough distance to appreciate all its subtleties could make it seem like a vice.

I like his dynamism, his lightness, his vibrations, his musical taste and the clarity of his words. But her practical teaching is very particular one might say... To help you understand, I can compare Uriel's teachings to a situation we all know well:

Many of us have a great friend who takes us out of our comfort zone by pushing us to try things we wouldn't even dare to do in our dreams...

At the time, we are a bit angry with him, but then we laugh heartily, like children... Uriel is that friend! The one who never let's go of our hand but who doesn't hesitate to push us into the water when we are afraid to dive!

His goal isn't to make a bad joke, he only wants us to knock out fear because our potential is superior. Did I feel better afterwards? Not really! After wisdom, action, so he wanted to shake me up a bit...

The inspiring light is the spear of faith that pierces the devil on earth…

I now understand that silence was a refuge from the lies, the unspoken things in my life. The ones from outside but especially the one coming from me. Perceiving the invisible and rejecting it, mockery or a spiritual world that was far too egocentric for my taste were the walls of my barricades. Building on a decoy...

When we don't find all the answers, we look for excuses or good reasons to hide. The inspiring light that Uriel mentioned in his advice introduces us to a new way of thinking, far from the ego and its meanderings... Take the last dusty corpses out of the cupboard and give them a decent burial. They too have a right to peace... Michael's support at the beginning of the coaching was invaluable to me as I was able to detach myself from the most disturbing patterns in relation to my loved ones. Doing and undoing to grow... Again, and again...
Uriel was not of my opinion, I had to claim victory too quickly because he revealed to me the aspect of a family problem that I thought I had exorcised...

Some of my relatives, when they get together, have a toxic habit of patting themselves on the back for great projects... When these meetings take place, I know that I expect hours of self-congratulation, an over-exposure of facts that do not exist in reality... Their discourse is so well-rehearsed that it develops an aura of overwhelming superiority and anxiety.

In the past, when I tried to share my ideas or dreams, I was automatically silenced with a *"Yes, but when I do this great thing, I'm talking about, it will be extraordinary"*.

Or they would speak louder than me, repeating word for word what I had just said... Taking credit for things that are not theirs, a specialty....

I was completely transparent! When I had to relive it recently, I was furious!

Had they not seen anything? Hadn't they noticed my change? I was going to explode and fight.

I knew that if I did that, there would be no constructive dialogue, but I wanted to silence their useless chatter. Suddenly my anger turned to euphoria, I deflated like a balloon. Their voices sounded like a distant echo, and I began to observe them in turn. Why confront them with their outdated methods? Perhaps they were happy like this, feeling strong within the four walls of their house.

I fought against an injustice that didn’t exist.
I would have taken them as they were from the start, I wouldn't have had to turn into a Don Quixote imitation.
By their attitude, the energetic circle they have created aims at naturally ejecting me. For my part, this aspect of their mentality annoys me to no end, so why try to prove to them that I can succeed... A true dialogue of deaf ears!
I was desperately trying to keep up with people with whom I have little in common. To be invisible to them is a fantastic boon!
They are interested in nothing, but their microcosm and I didn't see that I have all the freedom to realize myself without having to be exposed to their reductive judgements!

It wasn't me personally that they were trying to isolate, their masquerade was isolating themselves and preventing them appreciating the beauties of life. Being aware of this only increased my euphoria. I felt compassion for them, it came from the heart and my face lit up with a smile. My attention returned to the conversation, which no longer seemed so exasperating. I surrounded my loved ones with light and said goodbye.

I was peacefully walking down the street on my way home when I saw a coin on the floor. When I find one, I always pick it up and look at the year of issue. On this one it was stamped 2009... This period corresponded to the memories that led to my low energy and the fear that my projects would fall apart.
I clutched the coin tightly in my hand and thanked Uriel warmly. I didn't need to worry; everything would be OK... By first eradicating the family roots with Michael, I activated the power of the bearer of *"The Spear of Faith that pierces the devil on earth".* Light, divine gold is the material from which this spear was forged.
The fluid of Uriel that keeps at bay the evil demons that linger in the depths of our soul...

"He who wields it wisely will have access to knowledge, then the fire of the father will burn in him for eternity."

The episode of meeting my relatives and the joy that arose when I was about to argue with them made me see that knowledge is not just about evolving to end negative cycles.

We don't have to prove anything to anyone, even ourselves. If the shadow of worry is lurking around to make us falter, never forget the love that surrounds us. Another tactic of the shadow to bring us back under its sway is to focus our attention on the joyful moments of the past.

So, you'll think, how it's vicious? Because when we think of those happy times we had, it's always with regret... In the *"it was so much better before"* or *"I'll never experience that again"* way.

To cherish the happy memories without regret and to let ourselves be carried towards the best, is to become the forger of our own *"Spear of Faith"*. The gold, the raw material, is available to us already.

To carry the inspiring light of Uriel which feeds the brilliant fire of the father... To become invincible and claim our immortality!

I regret to say that it is sadly true, the joys of old will not return. At least not as we knew them. But those golden nuggets on the way were glimpses of all the future happiness's we will experience intensely...
A thousand times better and perfect for us! Closing some positive cycles to keep only the best is to accept past blessings and feed on them to inspire the vision of what we will receive. To erase the belief that such bliss will never occur again because bliss is eternal.

Coaching No. 13 - 13th letter

Receive the inspiring light

"I help you clarify; I help you understand, I help you get around obstacles..."
Archangel Uriel - 2021

The light coaching is almost over. This penultimate stage consists of the application of the awareness's acquired so far in case of a reappearance of the hurtful and reducing ego. You will also become familiar with Uriel, if you don't already know him a little. As a divine artist and poet, he has a perception of pure light.

All Divine beings are composed of it; however, Uriel represents the sensitivity of that light.

As such, he imbues us with the insight and analysis necessary to make us inspired beings, capable of finding solutions to a problem or a blocking reaction.

This exercise will connect you to this energy of grace and beauty. This mixture of finesse and lucidity that we need in the face of the ego that causes doubt, to never give up... If you are one of those who need tangible proof to be convinced of the effectiveness of the personal work you have done, then you will love Uriel!

Like a sun, he will enhance the blessings you have received by amplifying the power of Michael, Gabriel and Raphael. The inspiring light in combination with Michael's action cleanses negative

energies, mental pollution, hurtful ego, influence of others.
The inspiring light in combination with Gabriel's action increases immediate intuition, inner guidance, awakens curiosity, opens minds to different horizons, reveals additional potentials to be developed in this life: we have other strings to our bow, our library of skills and knowledge is enriched
The inspiring light in combination with Raphael's action gives a boost to the joy of living, vitality, amplifies the force of attraction, brings personal and material triumph...
You will integrate the splendid coordination that exists between the Archangels and use it for your achievement. Acting like a vitamin cocktail, it manifests in the form of great ideas that turn setbacks into success.

Polyvalent, it always guides you to the best version of yourself. With it, you take the opinions of others into consideration, you hear them, but you don't bend to their will. We see the other person without judgment, equal, human... We know where we want to go, our ego is not and cannot influence us negatively anymore.

No preparatory notes are needed to write this thirteenth letter. Being natural and fluent in your words will help Uriel to determine how to transmit the inspiring light to you. Expect signs!

In my case, you might have noticed that my initiation focused on the last grievances I faced and my reactions to them. That doesn't mean that you experience the same thing, he will read your heart to choose how to act with you.

His goal is your victory through knowledge. He wants you to go on your way with lightness and grace. His inspiring light will first discharge the negativity that does you no good. This clarity will dissolve the worries, anxieties, doubts and outdated patterns that weaken your wings and disturb your flight.

Sample letter

From:

Born:

"My dear Archangel Uriel,

You, the flame of God, so brilliant, so inspiring, I ask for your help in the penultimate stage of my evolutionary journey. I am the phoenix ready to rise from the ashes, I have integrated the teachings of Michael, Gabriel and Raphael into me. I am transformed in my body, my heart, my soul and today I ask your light to inspire me to succeed and overcome the traps of the ego:

-

-Express yourself freely, naturally, synthesize your evolutions and reactions.

-

Thank you for bringing out the gold mine that will enable me to forge my spear of faith. Thank you for making my inspiring light shine, which cleanses, transforms and neutralizes what is no longer. Thank you for keeping alive in me the sacred fire of the Father, the clarity of knowledge, the luminous ideas, the joy that transcends all.

I walk the sacred path that is mine, I release all pressure from the ego and the outside world. I am me, complete, competent, happy, bright, always inspired. I walk beside you on the path that leads to the Kingdom.
I radiate, in respect and humility.
I trust in you, in me, in us, in light and in inspiration!
Thank you, thank you, thank you! I love you!"

The Alchemist

"Then the formula will be yours and you shall be eternal among men…"
Archangel Uriel – June 2021

The deadline is coming...
Intuition assailed me without warning, happy to be able to express itself freely... I no longer must silence it or cultivate antagonism towards it... I have used her in the service of others with heart and precision for years, she is not my enemy… It is present, in its place... clear, limpid and in phase with what I have

become. Now, bad omens no longer frighten me because they belong to the person who receives them, to the mouth that interprets and pronounces them. There are no such things as infallible beings, because human issues always get involved... Don't give power to others and trust yourself, against all odds!

I felt a great change and the goal of the teaching was almost reached, the freedom that follows anxiety. The only question left in my mind was this:

"Unconsciously, you waited for such a transformation all your life, what do you choose to do with it?"

Having the Archangels by my side, benefiting from their wisdom reassured me, with them I could not fall, but what would happen when the time came for me to stand alone again?
Would I repeat some of my past mistakes?
I am convinced that this experience I was given with God's four most incredible allies made me different, I found ME while cleaning up my relationship with HIM and THEM.

In my heart I knew that they would support me no matter what! But inside my head, a nostalgic tune was playing... I wasn't ready to see them go, I still had so much to learn from them...

I was thinking about my life, the pieces of my story were coming together, and I had the strength to laugh at some moments that made me cry. Usually, the wise guidance of my strange friends led me to discovery.

I had become accustomed to being carried, protected by their immense wings, proportional to the size of their love.

I wanted to write Uriel, opening a little more to this friend who knew me so well!

I loved talking with them, and hearing what they had to tell me, simple truths that warm the heart and lighten the spirit…

- My beautiful Uriel, when the teaching of light is finished, what will happen? What comprehension do you have to give me for the future?

So, he answered:

"We have always been there! For all we will be there! You refuse to see yourself; you refuse to see the world; you contemplate the illusion. You fight against life, the one HE has given you! HE knows the abilities HE has assigned to you! HE sees, HE knows, HE understands, looking into the mirror of the Father! To face, humble, proud, the Divine reflection of indulgent acceptance…

The shadow turns away those who decide to follow it, living in the man who makes all faith perish. HIS truth distorted by the soothsayer's fancy, the purity marred by ill omen, the chimerical fight in the name of nothing.

HE has no will but yours, supporting the call of the heart that goes to him, the past time isn't like the time of tomorrow, opening the doors of destiny…

You have looked HIM in the face, our successive faces are his…

Then on the threshold of the Kingdom, as conflict rages one last time, within peace, your qualities are HIS qualities, there's no error, free choice, everything is, was and will be as planned…

Blessed, HE wants it, HE has wanted it, HE will want it for you, for all… HIS light, always, here, now, elsewhere, everywhere…
Glorifies by manifesting HIS life, YOUR life…
Man creates lack and separation whereas in the Kingdom all is connected… Transforming ignorance into truth then the Greatness of the Miracle will be perpetuated, honored, multiplied
You are HIM; he is YOU, the secret heritage of immortality"

Such words deserved my full attention.
Uriel was very effusive, and I didn't want to lose any of the precious dialogue.
My hand hastily transcribed the celestial dictation, which now appears on the front page of the notebook in which I collected all the conversations with Archangels.
Long before those words became daily messages that made me honor life in all circumstances, I read and reread each verse to become completely immersed in them. The magic of these words depends on one' s interpretation of them. Each will find a resonance

that opens the doors to dimensions that inspire and uplift.

The Divine contact that is established for those who are ready will be surprising, unique and personal. What Uriel told me made sense to conclude my healing, he didn't want me to forget the fundamentals of initiating journey I experienced with them. And most importantly, no matter what our life was, we have and will always have something to say, to accomplish…

Who are we? Who am I? Why am I here? Where do I belong?

…You have looked HIM in the face, our successive faces are his

Then on the threshold of the Kingdom, as conflict rages one last time, within peace

Your qualities are HIS qualities

There's no error, free choice, everything is, was and will be as planned… Blessed, HE wants it, HE has wanted it, HE will want it for you, for all…

HIS light, always, here, now, elsewhere, everywhere…

Glorifies by manifesting HIS life, YOUR life

Man creates lack and separation whereas in the Kingdom all is connected
Transforming ignorance into truth then the Greatness of the Miracle will be perpetuated, honored, multiplied
You are HIM; he is YOU, the secret heritage of immortality…

These questions that I asked myself many times are now answered!
I'm not my parents, I'm not the people who loved or hated me, I'm not what I believed I was...
I'm not my body, this envelope under which the world knows me as an individual... I'm much more than that, essence of time in perpetual motion, the spirit that stops to rest from its long journeys...
In the vastness of the Universe, we're the useful and blessed lights.
We're what we have always been, triumphant and free beings!
Golden nuggets to rediscover endlessly… Since I was a little girl, I was fascinated by extraordinary destinies, lost treasures, great acts of bravery... By those men and women who have transformed the world while

fighting to impose their ideas... Behind every success, every wealth, there is a story... From the corner where I was hiding, I was fed by these glorious examples that helped me to bear the dark hours... To each his moment, the wheel starts to turn again...

The lead fades away and surprise gold materializes... The revealed value, the eternal life in its authentic aspect. It shines, not from vanity because it doesn't care, but from acceptance... of being!

The magician, the miraculous, the alchemist who is at one with history and legend to find symbolic gold that no longer remains hidden...

So, repeat after me:

"I am the alchemist who turns every aspect of my life, past, present, future and more, into gold!"

Coaching No.14 - 14th letter

You are the alchemist of your life!

"Everything you're supposed to live, you lived it...
Everything you have left to live is yours...
When? yesterday, today, tomorrow because the formula is never the same.
You are eternity in the ephemeral..."
Archangel Uriel - 2021

Uriel holds your hand firmly to enter your Promised Land. So many miles traveled in search of this peaceful haven that awaited you...
It's finally here, in your sight, within you... Your soul is coming home. In this body and this life to which you have repeatedly declared war...
Shame, remorse or guilt no longer exist. You are the Alchemist, the scientist, the creator, the one who now knows that he will never be alone again wherever he goes. The one who knows that he can achieve anything because he has the necessary tools at his

disposal! This fourteenth letter concludes the light coaching. The foundations of the building are solid, time for new creations. What has just been accomplished is the spiritual work of a lifetime.

It's a time of experience and maturity: we realize that with age our reactions and our interpretation of facts change. Evolution is accessible to everyone and being a self-proclaimed lightworker doesn't change anything!

Lightworker... a meaningless term... Just a name that sounds good in society, but it defines nothing because light is everywhere, an eternal resource available to everyone...

From the homeless to the most eminent leader, it's present, inexorably... Spirituality is only one of the means to achieve it.

Changes continue to take place and remind us that our lives are meaningful and useful.

You, me, all of us, are the perfect links in the chain. We may sometimes despair that we cannot change the world, but we completely miss the fact that we contribute to making the world we are part of better.

And yet... If you weren't there, the world of many people who know you would be empty!
The alchemist, before mastering the transformation of metals to perfection, learned to gather the pieces of light to better reflect it.
To be proud of your life in its entirety is having the courage to say loud and clear:

"This is my life, I am perhaps not perfect, but I am here, rich in my experiences! Whether you like it or not!"

This is the secret of man's gold and eternal life, assume what you have done and who you are, in its entirety. Everything you have done, learned, understood, overcome!
Trusting your ability to turn every event in your life into a resounding success is the gift that Uriel now holds for you!
To reveal the powers of the alchemist within you, take pride in the fact that you are still standing despite the circumstances. You may think that the blows of fate have left you no choice, when you used them to your advantage without knowing it. You

moved forward instead of treading water. This is the theme of your letter: to explain all the things you have had to overcome in your life, which you can be proud of because it is part of your story.
It belongs to no one else and the way you have dealt with adversity defines your light footprint. You will also talk about all the internal and external factors that helped you to move forward, which never extinguished your flame...
It's important to create a luminous bridge between this past, which you have assumed with joy, and today. You will expose the projects of your heart and the ideas that will enable you to realize them.

By being fully aware of your resources, you will allow Uriel's energy to intensely nourish your inner fire, the flame that unites the miraculous power of the four Archangels with yours.
Absolute consecration!
Thus, you will always receive the inspiration that will lead you to success in the respect and light of your potential.

Sample letter

From:

Born:

"Dearest Archangel Uriel,

The past is no more, the old is swept away but my body, my heart and my soul of light remain. The metal is in fact gold... Pure, precious and rare!

The transformations have shaped me. I have grown, between joy and pain, but I regret nothing because the rhythm of life beats within me... Today, tomorrow, always... I realize all the treasures and qualities I have developed, sometimes even without my knowledge.

I have fought the hardest battle of all, the one that pitted me against myself:

-

Talk about personal victories over adversity, actions that have made you better, moments of pride and happiness that have allowed you to move forward, etc. Entrust future projects and current ideas to be carried out.

-

Uriel, my friend, beautiful Flame of God, thank you for being my beacon in the night and for blessing me with your light, the light that drives away all the shadows in and around me.

I am strong and proud of my experiences.

Through knowledge I have found my philosopher's stone, the jewel of growth and enlightenment that makes me fully love myself and my life, past, present and future. I fully inhabit my body, time and space.

Thank you for always keeping me on the right path that serves my highest good.

Thank you for always inspiring me in my life and projects. Thank you for turning my disadvantages into assets. I am happy, brilliant, miraculous.

I am the Alchemist who changes into gold what needs to be done, to spread the light in my promised land. I am Victory, I am Triumph!

I trust in you, in me, in us, in life, in my success!

The bond that unites me to the Kingdom of Heaven is unbreakable!

Thank you to all that exists and much more!

I love you!"

What can you hope for next? Everything is possible! Your days, nights, present and future are yours!
Every day of my life is made up of joys and if a problem arises, the solution to solve it presents itself "as by magic".

The blessings of the Alchemist and the energy of the Archangels are manifested in the small as well as in the big events of life, both for me and for those around me.
In the week following the letter, I felt in the mood to celebrate something without knowing exactly what. With some friends, we improvised a lunch in a new Parisian restaurant.
I was happy to share a meal in excellent company and to inaugurate the establishment's opening. The place, atmosphere, food, staff, everything was perfect! My friends and I were not disappointed with our choice... That was without counting the surprise awaiting us at the end...
When it came time to pay, I asked the waiter in charge of our table for the check and he told us that since we were among the first 100 customers, we

were entitled to free lunch. I felt so grateful, so pleased... I took my wallet from my bag and tipped our waiter 10 euros to thank him for his kindness.

We just had such a warm moment, I wanted to share somehow some of the joy that this unexpected gift brought. And as happiness never comes alone, one of my friends made a beautiful love encounter that day... Since then, events of this kind have been a frequent occurrence in my daily life. My spirits are high, my heart is in celebration…

What's the point of getting stuck in some projects? If we don't always know what life has in store for us, there's a good reason for that: to let in the unknown that is specially planned for each of us.
It's not the fall that we should fear, but the paralysis caused by the fear of falling. This should never stop us from following our hearts. The unexpected miracle happens from one minute to the next… Life makes us invincible... We don't really believe it, but so it is...
… Since the dawn of time!

Moment of Gratitude

"It's not a thank you, it's the beginning of a journey and a time of meeting…"

Archangel Uriel - 2021

The teaching of Archangels ends. Earth, Water, Air and Fire vibrate harmoniously together and are in osmosis with the possible. From where he sits, the Big Boss looks at us, proud of his children and what they have traversed to get to him.

After the past year, I seemed to wake up from a dream. I wondered how I would do without the daily company of my friends. They did for me what no one else had ever done before and for that I am eternally grateful…

But I felt sad... After the Alchemist's exercise, when I put my letter in the envelope for Uriel, big tears started rolling down my cheeks. I was a child again, afraid to be abandoned! How silly! They were there, all I had to do was write and think about them and they arrived...

To thank Uriel and all others for their light, I organized a day of rest by the sea.
Walking and playing in the sand, hearing the waves lapping on the shore, admiring the sea that stretches away to the horizon in this landscape not yet invaded by tourists... I was delighted by this sight!

Nature in its most beautiful and dearest to my heart… This graceful moment, I offered it to the Archangels. I gave them my newfound joy of a little girl who loves collecting shells. I gifted them every hour of the day, from sunrise to sunset... In homage to our friendship, not far from the waves, I wrote our names in the sand... I sat in front of my improvised fresco and looked to the horizon thinking of them.

Far away, over the water, a large and familiar white shape appeared. I put my hand on my chest and sent him all the love I felt at that moment... We would never leave now!
The waves finally washed our names away... Michael, Gabriel, Raphael, Uriel, Isa... The nature's miracle, the perfection that unites visible and invisible... This isn't

a farewell, just a goodbye... Thank you very much, for the time we have spent together and the time we have left.

Thanks for all!

CHAPTER 18

The Power of Four

"Whatever you ask, we will give you more..."
Michael, Gabriel, Raphael and Uriel Archangels
– 2021

You are now familiar with the individual energy of Michael, Gabriel, Raphael and Uriel.
You have discovered or re-discovered the unlimited possibilities of their abilities on your whole being during the light coaching. Now you can abandon the crutches and walk normally again. You no longer need instructions and guidance to write to our friends in the light. You can now use all your creativity to expand your correspondence with them.

If a question arises in relation to a choice to be made, an encounter, a daily challenge and you still doubt your intuition, the Archangels will work together to bring you the appropriate guidance.

They are present to accompany you every day when you need their support.

Never forget: *You thought you were weak, but you never needed crutches, only to integrate the truth of your personal sovereignty.*

Individually, they work wonders. Collectively, they work miracles!

Some situations cannot be understood from one point of view. This part is dedicated to the requests for which you will call upon pairs of Archangels. For energetic reasons, I advise you to have them work in pairs in order to obtain better indications. Indeed, to call upon too many divine entities at the same time can create "interference" in the help received.

To help you visualize what I'm getting at, I'll give you an example: You ask Michael for help, but you realize that your situation also requires Uriel's intervention, you tell him your problem and you realize again that Raphael could also do something... In the long run, your request is so modified that it doesn't resemble what it was originally!

However, up there they have already started working on what you wanted to know in the first place. Each new request you send requires adjustments on their side and "delays" the arrival of the answer you might get. To collaborate productively, follow your instincts and don't hesitate to set up stages to your requests. When you have received the answers, you ask for additional information and so on...

To remain in a dynamic of autonomy and reflection, I advise you, when you form your duos of Archangels, to choose one who will work on matter and the other on the intellect. Thus, you will be able to obtain a global guidance.

It will be easier for you to visualize where you are in relation to the situation that concerns you. This will allow you to act calmly and effectively. For example, Michael and Raphael will act more quickly on matter. Gabriel and Uriel will be more sensitive to the subtle and intellectual spheres.

The exceptional cases where you can write letters to Michael, Gabriel, Raphael and Uriel at the same time are:

- Thanks, gratitude for life, help obtained
- Apply for protection
- If you find yourself temporarily in a bind and you do not know which of the four would be the most suitable to act with you.

Remember that your intuition is your best compass, listen to it!

When I'm concerned, I no longer fixate on what I'm worried about.
I analyze the big picture and think about how best to approach the Archangels. I then hear who I need to write to in order to move forward. Never reject instinct in favor of logic!
It's not necessary to be a great psychic to be intuitive!
Trust yourself, on this earth you are the only one who knows what is good for you.
As with the correspondences of the light coaching, you will explain why you are asking for help and the episode in your life that leads you to this.
Always remain yourself, in all circumstances.

Letting anxieties get the better of you can disturb the interpretation of the divine guidance you receive.
In these cases, you must always be attentive to your body's reactions, as it will always guide you towards the truth that you need to know yours and the one that heaven wants to teach you.
God's emissaries can help you with many problems.

In this section you will find practical information about which pair of Archangels to turn to in certain situations. You can use the statements in your letters or write them on a piece of paper that you keep with you (in your pocket, for example).
The Archangel who appears first in your request represents the main force that will act on the whole situation. The second Archangel will frame the work of the first and bring his own skills to bear on the whole situation.
For example:
You want to find true love to build a lasting relationship. In this case, you would turn to Gabriel and Raphael. Logic would dictate that the primary force dealing with this issue is Raphael, given his

quick action in the matter. But Gabriel is the one who knows and relays God's decisions, so he will be the one to ensure the priority of your request. As your submission is quite legitimate, he will transmit to Raphael the circumstances to be put in place so that the meeting takes place perfectly in our dimension.

In any Divine and Archangelic intervention, there is necessarily a phase of interiorization and rise of consciousness. The light coaching has given you back your personal sovereignty so this preparatory mental stage should be short. The materialization in the real world should go smoothly as you now know what is good for you. Always keep in mind that the Archangels will guide you and help you in your daily life, but you are free to seize the opportunities that come your way or not. Don’t put any pressure on yourself!

If your consciousness doesn’t resonate with what is being sent to you, our friends of light will never leave you in the dark. They will adjust the circumstances to your current spiritual opening. Their priority is your comfort in life, so keep faith and trust!

CHAPTER 19

The Power of Four: Some practical situations

"Anytime call us, then you will hear our voices in your soul..."

Archangel Gabriel – 2020

Receiving guidance on a person's sincerity - Gabriel and Uriel

This type of request can help you when your intuition warns you about someone, but the person's attitude seems harmless. Gabriel will accentuate your instincts by sending you signs that will confirm whether you are getting the wrong idea. Uriel, a luminous diplomat, will guide you towards the best attitude to adopt.

"Dearest Gabriel and Uriel, you know the souls and the role they must play in my life. Thank you for helping me to discern whether the intentions of ... (name the person concerned) towards me are sincere. Thank you for directing me to the most appropriate response to restore light and balance between me ... and ... for our greater good!

I trust you; I trust myself; I trust us!

Thank you, thank you, thank you. So be it!"

Easing a conflict - Michael and Uriel

This sublime duo (the liberator and the scout) will defuse a conflict between you and someone you care about. Michael will release the roots of misunderstanding that are at the root of the conflict and Uriel will transform the surrounding negative energies so that calm can be restored gently.

"Dearest Michael and Uriel, you wish only for peace and love among men. The conflict I am currently experiencing with ... (name the person) is affecting me

greatly. Thank you for releasing me from the emotional burdens that have caused the conflict with ... Thank you for extinguishing the fire of harmful and contradictory feelings within me and redirecting me to serenity and light. Thank you for bringing out the peace that must be in this situation, for the good of all. I trust you; I trust myself; I trust us! Thank you, thank you, thank you. So be it!"

Freeing yourself from a negative imprint - Raphael and Gabriel

To be used when faced with aggression or other negative feelings from another person. Also works in cases of toxicity or vampirism.

Raphael will unburden and soothe your heart of accumulated negativity.

Gabriel will give you the strength to step back and overcome the emotional shock.

"Dearest Raphael and Gabriel, guardians of life,
I feel weakened by the negative reaction I have been facing.
Thank you for healing and healing the emotional rifts that this situation has left in my heart. Thank you for restoring and strengthening my energy with your divine waves so that I can transform this unpleasant experience into soothing light.
I let go of this negativity that does not belong to me, for my own good and that of all.
I trust you; I trust myself; I trust us!
Thank you, thank you, thank you. So be it!"

Making positive contacts

Raphael and Uriel

If you wish to expand your circle of friends, your professional network, meet people who are in tune with your consciousness plan, receive beneficial help in your endeavors. Raphael will attract opportunities to help you meet people and Uriel's light will ensure that the spiritual, mental and emotional connection is enriching and helpful to everyone's path.

"Dearest Raphael and Uriel,
A major element of life, social relationships enrich and elevate us. Thank you for guiding me towards positive encounters that will help me evolve in my present. Thank you for illuminating and enriching these encounters with love, understanding, respect and mutual support. For the good of all those concerned. I trust you; I trust myself; I trust us!
Thank you, thank you, thank you. So be it!"

Find love - Gabriel and Raphael

Love is the most important area of our existence. Finding a partner with whom you can build, and grow is one of the most important quests in life. Vibrating love is a gift and Gabriel, as God's messenger, knows perfectly well the Father's plans for our lives. So, he knows who you should meet, how and when. Raphael will accentuate your love attraction to open you up to the manifestation of this important encounter in the best possible conditions.

"Dearest Gabriel and Raphael, our Lord does not like to know that his children are alone, that is why he has provided a half for each of them.
Thank you for preparing my heart, my soul and my life to receive the love that is foreseen for me by our Father.
Thank you for raising my love attraction to the level of this love that I receive in my life.
I welcome with open arms the unconditional love that enriches both our souls, our paths meet, our hands hold and never let go. I love you and I bless you wherever you are. I trust you; I trust myself; I trust us! Thank you, thank you, thank you. So be it!"

Stopping self-sabotage

Michael and Raphael

At first glance, the effects of self-sabotage may seem like an occult attack. The sole instigator of this flood of negativity is the ego!
It gradually loses control and in order to regain its place in the individual's consciousness, it is capable of staging events worthy of the cinema, causing significant psychological damage: fatigue, loss of self-confidence, isolation, obstacles, etc. The illusion is so successful that the "victim" ends up believing in a negativity that does not exist. The powerful duo of Michael and Raphael will take you away from this vicious circle created from scratch.

"Dearest Michael and Raphael, powerful healers of consciousness, thank you for freeing me from the chains of my mental prison.
Thank you for transmuting these erroneous ego patterns into waves of light that cleanse and illuminate my consciousness.

Thank you for all this peace and love that balances me perfectly. I am back in reality, here and now, in perfect safety. I am in my place and on the right path. The mirages of the ego no longer exist, I send them into the light. The shadows dissipate and my life returns to normal. I trust you; I trust myself; I trust us!
Thank you, thank you, thank you. So be it!"

Feel the Sacred Joy

Uriel and Raphael

Along with love, joy is one of the greatest sources of radiance. These two emotions usually go hand in hand. High vibrations of joy form a powerful shield of protection around you. Feeling it in your heart and externalizing it maintains an optimal connection between you and the divine.
Uriel is responsible for spreading this joy within everyone, it is the healthy and stable inner fire.

Raphael, with his healing abilities, will create a space in your heart for this powerful wave to live.

"Dearest Uriel and Raphael, God has created for me an essence in His image, pure and perfect. Thank you for feeding my inner fire with the sacred joy that protects. Thank you for anchoring it firmly in my heart, that the light of my soul radiates at every moment and forms a shield of light around me.
I carry, I live, I always transmit the sacred joy now and for all times. For my good and that of others.
I trust you; I trust myself; I trust us! Thank you, thank you, thank you. So be it!"

Ask for financial abundance

Two Steps

The intentions behind this type of request must be clear and from the heart. The Archangels will ensure that your material desires are based on a sincere desire to do good to yourself and to others. If you need money because of a complex, arrogance, to show off, to please fools... Beware!

Heaven is generous, it will open the floodgates of abundance for a time to check what use you make of it. But if it finds that you abuse any power, you will receive a lesson in understanding in return.

Achieving financial abundance requires method and preparation.

Gabriel and Michael are the Archangels to ask for support in the first instance.

Again, Gabriel knows the nature of the financial abundance intended for you, the circumstances under which it is to come into your life, when you are ready to receive it... Everything you get will be aligned with your Life Mission, which will multiply the blessings afterwards.

Michael will take care of the whole earthly liberation part, that means the patterns you have regarding abundance, the false roads you take to reach it, the personal blocks that keep you away from it...

"Dearest Gabriel and Michael, Heaven generously provides for all our material needs.
Thank you for aligning me with the financial abundance in my life plan, I am grateful for the inexhaustible material resources that are available to me. Thank you for freeing me from the patterns, beliefs and blind alleys that limit my financial abundance here below. What no longer serves my good is sent out into the light and returned to me in the form of blessings.
I trust you; I trust myself; I trust us!
Thank you, thank you, thank you! So be it!"

Raphael and Uriel will combine their respective abilities to create opportunities that will empower you to achieve financial abundance.
These small, shiny pebbles strategically placed at specific points on your itinerary will build confidence in your ability to manifest the gifts of heaven.
You will only have to bend down to pick them up because they will be truly yours. Your heart will rejoice to see its true desires fulfilled.

"Dearest Raphael and Uriel, your divine creativity is limitless in supporting me on the path of abundance that is mine. Thank you for the new day that is dawning on my financial situation, I easily recognize the gifts you place in my path. Thank you for my financial needs being met. Money flows freely and comes to me easily now, in all circumstances. Thank you for your unconditional support and generosity to me, prosperity is mine for my sake and that of all. I trust you; I trust myself; I trust us!
Thank you, thank you, thank you! So be it!"

Cancel negative attacks

Two Steps

Life sometimes brings us face to face with "enemies" whose ego is such that it wreaks havoc on others. Most of the time, the destructive energy that these people show towards us is motivated by unhappiness, jealousy, pride, envy, cowardice... Not wishing to face their problems, nor to admit their self-hatred, they find "easy targets" to attack. We then enter a vicious circle that pits us against our oppressor.

By trying to defend ourselves, by being afraid, a power game is established and the struggle of good versus evil begins. Negative or occult attacks require mental preparation before any action can be taken to neutralize them. Dealing with this type of problem requires two steps.

The first is to rise above the belief that the curse itself is evil (whatever its origin).

For this, the Archangel pair to ask for help will be Raphael and Gabriel.

Healing power of Raphael will lighten the external energy loads that are weighing on you and restore emotional relief. Gabriel will mediate the situation by activating divine arbitration.

The strength he will transmit to you will stop the belief that the other person has all the power over you.

"Dearest Raphael and Gabriel, no man can boast of divine powers. Grace blesses the righteous and teaches

the slanderous. Thank you for unburdening my energy and my consciousness of all that does not vibrate the light. Thank you for leading to liberation the suffering souls who wish me harm, thank you for guiding me and keeping me on the path of sacred wisdom. Nothing can take away my sovereignty, I am protected, at peace, in tune with my Mission. I trust you; I trust myself; I trust us! Thank you, thank you, thank you! So be it!"

Time and experience have taught me that the strength of a negative attack really depends on the power you give it. Thinking you are just a puppet whose strings the oppressor deftly pulls only feeds his fictitious authority.

The one who inflicts evil is a slave to his demons, he tries to lock his target in the same prison... I am aware that it is easier said than done, but in case of an attack NEVER forget that nothing and nobody can deprive us of our light!

Without minimizing the impact that the actions of others can have on us, being aware of our personal sovereignty no longer subjects us to narrow wills. Now you can ask Uriel and Michael to finish the job.

It is customary for energies to go back to the sender... In your desperate attempt to protect yourself, you automatically put yourself in the position of a revenant: you want to heal evil with evil.
Uriel will surround you with his light and Michael will be responsible for freeing you and your "enemy". Thus, the battle ends…

"Dearest Uriel and Michael, justice and fairness always triumph. You alone in the divine realm are the impartial and benevolent judges of the events of our lives. Thank you for surrounding me with a halo of powerful light that no shadow can penetrate. Thank you for freeing me and my enemies from the battles that oppose us. Low instincts are replaced by love, joy and knowledge. May each of us be taught what we need to be taught in order to grow and advance in dignity. I am free from tyranny, now and forever!
I trust you; I trust myself; I trust us! Thank you, thank you, thank you! So be it!"

These few examples are part of the worries of everyday life, it is now your turn to adapt these generalities to your personal history. If you don't seek to harm, if love and neutrality direct your heart, you can be sure that the Archangels will support you intellectually and materially.

The links you will forge with them will be marvelous, unique... And your discoveries grandiose! Be proud of your truth, of your creativity, of your intuition...

Be your peace, be your strength and launch yourself!

CHAPTER 20

Epilogue

"Before life we were, during life we are, in eternity we remain..."

Archangel Gabriel – 2021

To this day, I still write letters to my friends Michael, Gabriel, Raphael and Uriel.

I no longer wait for specific instructions from them, I just tell them about my days, the trivialities of everyday life, the joys, the sorrows...

I know that they continue to be with me in my days and nights. I embrace their guidance with respect, only they know the itinerary...

The happiness of reunion is constantly renewed, as when we return from a long journey, and we are happy to hug our loved ones. When the feeling of finally coming home is stronger than the one that made us leave...

I'm a happy adult, I dance, I laugh, I dare, I create... I live, as if it were the first time... The child came back to her hill, she climbed her dear mountain... At the top, they were all there, her missing ones, her beautiful white angel and all her friends. Like her, they were smiling, they were at peace…

Together, they surrounded her with their love because in the end, we spend our existence chasing time but in the end it's all we have left... When it rains, I lean against the window to watch the rain fall. And if the thunder rumbles, I sometimes raise my eyes to the sky to watch God screeching at the unwise children.

I smile at this short-lived anger because the old man is profoundly good, our foolishness keeps him eternally young. He has a love for us that only he knows...

Every morning I raise my cup of coffee and toast to this new day. I bless the twists and turns; I no longer dread the dark forests I had to go through. The darkness has dissipated, it was only mirages in my desert to prevent me from discovering my green oasis, my promised land... I'm free...

Maybe that was the wrath of God, the tears of Jesus and the rainy days. When time has done its work, when the cycle closes, and the sun can shine again. When you realize that the trials and tribulations of life are wonderful gifts that take you to places and people you have never seen before...

I carried this book like a baby, now it no longer belongs to me. I let go of its hand so that it can learn to walk and follow its own path...

Go forward without fear, always keeping in mind the value you have in you. You are one of the wonders that this world is happy to welcome.

May your destiny be beautiful, your present and your future radiant. Try, dare, be, go, live and become...

Never fear the depths of the precipice, spread your wings to fly away into this eternity which belongs to you and is only waiting for you... Now and forever! Amen!

Thanks...

For me, writing this book was a real challenge!
I carried this desire in my heart for years, constantly postponing the moment of manifesting it in matter...
I was afraid... Of not being able to write it, of simply not being able to do it!
I would first like to thank the world of light, for all the inspiration and love they have given me in my life. I thank Michael, Gabriel, Raphael, Uriel and our Father, my Dream Team, for showing me the way and guiding me through the creative journey of writing this book.
Thank you for their presence at my side in the here and now, in the yesterday and tomorrow... Without their strength, I would never have come out of my shell and put these words on paper.
Thank you to my loved ones. They can be counted on the fingers of one hand and even if our relationships were not always perfect, they will stay with me, against all odds...
I dedicate a huge loving thought to my dogs: Bernie, my son; Ernesto Guevara, the patriarch; Leo and

Margaret, the infernal tandem. Seeing them live and evolve daily constantly reminds me of the love that floods this earth, if we take the trouble to notice it.

Those who have loved me will always be in my heart, but I also make room for those who have hurt me, betrayed me or done me wrong. Without them, I probably wouldn't have learned any valuable lessons. Blessings and gratitude to all those people who helped me get to where I am today. They are proof that nothing is insurmountable!

Finally, a huge thank you to you who took the time to read me. Without readers, a book doesn't exist and its author even less, so thank you from the bottom of my heart for having let us enter your life, the Archangels and me, for a moment... of eternity!

Love and Light

Isa

About the author

Isa Millot is a French psychic and healer, a profession she has practiced for many years. Today she devotes herself to writing and coaching with the aim of helping others to develop their highest potential.

Follow me on social networks:

Instagram: @archangelscoffee

Facebook: @archangelscoffee

TABLE OF CONTENTS

Printed by Lightning Source – 1, Ingram BLVD,
La Vergne TN – USA

Legal deposit: August 2022

CPSIA information can be obtained
at www.ICGtesting.com
Printed in the USA
LVHW081353060922
727630LV00008B/405

9 782958 411114